MW00999095

360

Petal Play

THE TRADITIONAL WAY

by
Joan Shay

American Quilter's Society
P. O. Box 3290 • Paducah, KY 42002-3290
www.AQSquilt.com

Located in Paducah, Kentucky, the American Quilter's Society (AQS) is dedicated to promoting the accomplishments of today's quilters. Through its publications and events, AQS strives to honor today's quiltmakers and their work and to inspire future creativity and innovation in quiltmaking.

EDITOR: BARBARA SMITH
GRAPHIC DESIGN: ELAINE WILSON
COVER DESIGN: MICHAEL BUCKINGHAM
PHOTOGRAPHY: CHARLES R. LYNCH

Library of Congress Cataloging-in-Publication Data
Shay, Joan
    Petal play the traditional way / Joan Shay
       p. cm.
     ISBN 1-57432-770-4
    1. Appliqué--Patterns. 2. Patchwork--Patterns. 3. Flowers in art.
    4. Patchwork quilts. 5. Fusible materials in sewing.   I. Title.
    TT779 .S4823 2001
    746.46'041--dc21

                   2001003134

Additional copies of this book may be ordered from the American Quilter's Society, PO Box 3290, Paducah, KY 42002-3290, or online at www.AQSquilt.com.

Copyright © 2001, Joan Shay

All rights reserved. No part of this book may be reproduced, stored in any retrieval system, or transmitted in any form, or by any means including but not limited to electronic, mechanical, photocopy, recording, or otherwise, without the written consent of the author and publisher. Patterns may be copied for personal use only.

Dedication

"A dream is a wish your heart makes."

This book is dedicated to my husband, Tony, who always makes my dreams come true.

I love you.

Acknowledgments

The greatest gift of life is friendship, and I have received it.
Hubert Humphrey

A heartfelt thank you to...

my family, friends, and students, who have supported me unconditionally;

my son Matt, my daughter Kristin, her husband, Jon, and my granddaughter, Shay, for enriching my life;

Jo Coon for her "gentle" prodding;

Adelaide Chandler for her proofreading skills;

Sharlene Jorgensen, Betty Kiser, and Pat Yamin for sharing their special techniques with me;

Kim Emperato for accepting my desperate calls with computer questions;

Mary Hayes, Adie Chandler, Peg Bell, Wendy Strumwasser, Judy Irish, Judy Allen, and Jackie Davis for their assistance;

Carla Callahan whose wonderful sense of humor made some days tolerable;

Barbara Smith for her careful guidance; and

AQS and Meredith Schroeder for allowing my garden to continue to bloom.

Contents

My Garden Continues to Bloom

I had completed a four-block Double Wedding Ring top and was deciding on a quilting pattern when I realized the rings made perfect frames for my Appli-bond magnolia flowers. The whole idea had a romantic feel, and I excitedly proceeded.

While working on this quilt, the concept of combining other traditional blocks and my Appli-bond flowers began to intrigue me. Many patterns, such as the Double Wedding Ring or Lady of the Lake, have large vacant centers. They are perfect for incorporating the Appli-bond flowers directly into the design. Other patterns, such as Nosegay, require alternating the traditional blocks with Appli-bond flower blocks. It's also lovely to appliqué the flowers directly on a completed block like the Log Cabin. It's fun to relate the flower to the block name, but it's not always necessary.

I decided to propose a challenge to many of my former students and friends. I asked them to combine a traditional block with one of the flowers from my Petal Play pattern line or from a pattern in my previous book, *Petal by Petal* (AQS, 1998). Some of the exciting results are pictured on pages 101–108.

I now extend this challenge to you. Use the Appli-bond patterns as presented in this book, or mix and match the flowers with these or other traditional quilt patterns. I hope you will have as much fun as my friends and I have had in creating quilts with *Petal Play the Traditional Way*.

Chapter 1
GENERAL INSTRUCTIONS

The quilt patterns in this book combine traditional blocks with some of my new Appli-bond flower designs. In some instances, the flowers need to be appliquéd before the quilt blocks are sewn together; for example, see Forget-me-not and Queen Anne's Lace (page 58). In other cases, the quilt must be constructed first, as with the Magnolia (page 36). It's fun to create unique quilts by combining pieced blocks and Appli-bond appliqué.

In Appli-bond, two or more pieces of fabric are fused together. I have found that it is necessary to use HeatnBond® UltraHold iron-on adhesive for this process, because other bonding agents will allow fraying. The stiffened appliqué pieces have no turn-under allowances, and the edges need no further finishing. The pieces are tacked down, usually in the centers, with various embroidery stitches, while the edges remain free, creating a realistic three-dimensional effect. Flowers that can be difficult to create with traditional appliqué methods are easily accomplished with Appli-bond.

Here are some things to keep in mind as you use the patterns:
• The cutting instructions for the pieced blocks include ¼" seam allowances.
• The turn-under allowances for needle-turn appliqué are generally ³⁄₁₆" and are cut by eye. Remember, you do not need a turn-under allowance for Appli-bond. Cut all bonded pieces on the line.
• All yardage is figured on 42"-wide fabric, which is the useable width after selvages have been removed.
• Always remove the selvage. It should not be included in a block or appliqué piece.
• The lengthwise grain runs parallel to the edge of the fabric. Crosswise grain runs from selvage to selvage. Both are considered straight grain.
• True bias is cut at a 45-degree angle. It is the stretchiest fabric grain. Most bias cuts for the flowers and stems do not have to be true bias. Cut the pieces slightly off grain so they will curve easily. See bias instructions on page 14.

FABRIC SELECTIONS

When you are making an appliqué quilt, two types of fabrics are needed, background and appliqué. In selecting your fabrics, choose 100-percent cotton because polyester will not hold a sharp crease, and it is more likely to fray. Purchase fabrics with a high thread count and avoid any loose weaves, which will fray.

Background fabrics need not be limited to white or ecru. Be creative. You can use printed, multicolored, and hand-dyed fabrics. You might also consider muted plaids, pastels, or blacks. Dark backgrounds create a dramatic feel.

Unless you plan to wash the finished quilt, it's best not to pre-wash your fabrics because the sizing applied by the manufacturer helps to stabilize the appliqué pieces. If the fabrics are properly bonded, there will be no fraying, and curled fabrics will stay curled. (See page 12 for information on curling.)

I do not pre-wash, but you can do what suits your needs. You can still wash and dry these quilts after they have been made, even if the fabrics were not pre-washed. However, it is important to check fabrics for bleeding before you use them. This can be done simply by cutting a small swatch of fabric and placing it in a clear glass of water for a few minutes. Let the fabric swatch dry on a white piece of similar fabric. If the white fabric is stained, the swatch fabric is unsuitable for that project.

The larger the variety of colors and shades you use, the more interesting the finished quilt will be. Tone-on-tone fabrics (those having more than one color or shade but which read as one color from a distance) add texture, and the shading adds to the realism. Hand-dyed gradations are also recommended because they are effective for shading.

Consider using the wrong sides of fabrics, which are generally a little lighter. Use solid colors sparingly. They can be boring if overused. Bonding two different fabrics together adds interest. Real flower petals and leaves are

not the same shade on both sides.

Audition your fabrics. Make a fabric paste-up of your block and check the color placement. Remember that real flowers are generally darker in the center and gradually become lighter toward the edges.

SUPPLIES

Scissors

You will need two pairs of scissors, one to use exclusively for fabric and one for paper and template material. Small embroidery scissors with sharp points are also recommended because they are helpful for maneuvering around small curves.

Spring-action scissors decrease fatigue during cutting. With traditional scissors, the ring around your thumb is what causes discomfort. Spring-action scissors do not have a thumb ring.

Rotary cutters

A rotary cutter looks like a pizza cutter, but it is much sharper. Used in combination with an acrylic ruler, it allows you to cut single or multiple layers of fabric quickly and accurately. Because the blade is very sharp, it needs to be handled carefully.

There are many different sizes of blades. The small

blade is beneficial for cutting curved appliqué pieces. Use a pinking rotary-cutting blade on bonded fabric to achieve a ruffled effect.

Appli-bond needles

When I first started doing Appli-bond appliqué, I attached the bonded pieces to the background by using an embroidery needle. This was often difficult, especially when stitching through several thicknesses. I have since discovered better needles. They have three cutting edges and easily pierce the bonded fabric. The eye of the needle accommodates two strands of embroidery floss. A third strand can be added if you use a needle threader. You won't want to use the needles for traditional appliqué however. They are too sharp and will cut the fabric. These needles are also helpful when doing a button hole stitch around a fused shape as in fusible appliqué. Try them when working with ultra suede, you will be very pleased. (See Home Shopping, page 109.)

Straw (milliner's) needles

Straw needles, also called milliner's needles, are longer and finer than the traditional appliqué needle, which is known as a "sharp." The extra length helps in needle-turning the edges of the appliqué pieces. The thinness of the needle allows you to take a smaller bite of the fold when appliquéing, thus improving your stitch because the thread will not be as visible. I use a #10 straw needle.

Embroidery needles

An embroidery needle is used to embroider unbonded fabric. It has a long narrow eye that easily accommodates floss.

Threads

When appliquéing, it is desirable that the stitches not show, so the thread color should match the appliqué piece, not the background fabric. One-hundred percent cotton thread is recommended. However, you can use a poly-cotton blend if the color match is better. Gray thread will often blend with most colors. Choose a darker thread rather than a lighter one if you cannot match perfectly. The darker thread will show less. Here is an easy way to remember this: "If you want a seam and not a marker, choose a thread a little darker."

Always thread the needle with the part of the thread that comes off the spool first and knot it where you cut it. Threads are made by twisting many fibers together. If you thread your needle in this manner, you will decrease the number of knots.

Nylon thread is necessary when working with beads. I recommend size D.

Embroidery floss

Embroidery floss has six strands per skein. Cut the floss to a workable length, no longer than 18". Separate the strands by pulling one strand at a time, straight up and out of the skein. This eliminates twisting. When using multiple strands, always separate the strands first and then put them back together to increase the volume of the floss, making the stitches fuller. Each pattern instructs you on the number of strands necessary for a particular embroidery stitch. Combining two different shades of floss creates an interesting effect.

Beads

French knots are really easy. (See page 19 for the instructions.) You can, however, replace French knots with beads, if you prefer. Some of the flowers are embellished with beads, which really emphasizes the texture.

Here are some things to remember when purchasing beads:

• Use glass beads. Remember you will probably be ironing over them, and plastic beads will melt.

• Make sure your Appli-bond or straw needle can fit through the opening.

• A ceramic bead dish, sold in bead stores, is helpful for handling small beads. Ceramic is preferable to plastic because plastic creates static.

Basting glue

I often position my bonded pieces with basting glue rather than stab stitches. It's much faster, and the position can be changed easily. Look for a water-soluble glue tube with a tiny applicator so the glue can be released one drop at a time. Place the glue where you would stitch, not along the edges, so that the edges will still lift from the background. The piece will be held firmly until moistened or washed. (See Home Shopping, page 109.)

Markers

There are many marking tools available, choose whichever type you like best. Remember to test for removability. With Appli-bond, the petals lift off the background, so it is essential that no marks remain. Whenever possible, I use a thin-line blue, water-soluble pen for light fabrics. I like this type of marker because it is forgiving. If your appliqué piece doesn't quite cover the line, the line can be erased with water. I have had no problems with this pen, but you need to test each fabric to make sure the marker can be completely removed. Do not iron the markings or leave the piece in the sun because heat will set the marks. Remove all the markings before the quilt top is layered and before a piece is curled. To erase the markings, use a cotton swab moistened with cold water.

Fine-line mechanical pencils, .5 mm, make accurate marking tools also, and wax-free white chalk pencils are useful for marking dark fabrics. If you are using a pencil, be sure to sharpen it often so that the point remains fine. Again, test each fabric and each type of marker to make sure that you can see the markings and remove them easily.

Saral paper

Saral paper is a useful product for marking dark fabrics. It is a wax-free, transfer paper that comes in many colors, similar to dressmaking paper. To use this product, place your fabric on a hard surface, right side up. Lay a piece of saral paper, colored side down, on the fabric and place the design to be traced on top. Trace the design lines with a sharp pencil. The image will be transferred to the fabric. The paper can be reused many times. The markings can be erased like pencil lead or removed by washing.

Sandpaper board

A board covered with sandpaper and placed under your fabric will prevent it from slipping as you mark. For an inexpensive and portable sandpaper board, glue a piece of sandpaper to a manila folder.

Templates

See-through templates need to be made for each different pattern piece. Use a plastic that does not have a grid because grid lines will interfere with your ability to see the fabric pattern. See-through templates are especially helpful for isolating a desired motif from a large-print fabric.

To make a see-through template, trace the pattern on the plastic and mark all necessary information on the right side of the template. Label templates with a fine-line permanent marker. Record the pattern name, letter, block size, grain line, and number of pieces. It is important to identify the right side so that you do not reverse a template by mistake. A template-marking pencil, available in fabric stores, is helpful because it marks clearly and does not rub off. Cut the templates on the line. There is no seam allowance.

Store the templates, separated by flower or block, in re-sealable plastic bags. Reinforce one side of the bag with clear packing tape, punch holes in it, and place it in a small three-ring binder. Arrange the bags alphabetically so you can locate your templates easily. These bags will become the start of your flower library.

To prepare your pieces for appliqué, trace the outline of the templates on the right side of the fabric with the appropriate marker. Whenever possible, place your templates on the bias. The pieces will lie flatter, and the curves will turn more smoothly.

Here are some things to keep in mind when working with templates:

• The pattern pieces are all full-size.

• Arrows on a pattern represent the grain line.

• Accuracy is very important.

Design wall

A design wall is a helpful tool. To make one for your sewing room, cover a piece of foam core (available in art or office supply stores) with flannel and attach it to a wall. Appliquéd pieces and whole blocks will adhere to the flannel without being pinned. If you use a design wall as you construct the appliqué flowers or pieced blocks, you can step back and preview the color, size, and placement of fabrics. If you are not satisfied, the pieces can easily be rearranged or exchanged.

APPLI-BOND APPLIQUÉ

In the Appli-bond appliqué method, two fabric layers are used for each bonded motif, such as a leaf or petal. The two fabrics are bonded, wrong sides together, before the motif is cut. Cut the motif on the line, leaving no allowances. Then attach the motif in place with embroidery stitches, creating a three-dimensional effect. You can bond the same fabric for both layers or you can use two different fabrics. To increase the 3-D effect, try a darker color for the back of the motif.

These dimensional pieces maintain their shapes even when washed and dried, and fraying will not occur if the fabrics have been bonded properly. Appli-bond appliqué can be combined with traditional appliqué to create beautifully realistic flowers and leaves.

Let's bond

Here is some general information to help you when bonding fabrics:
• Iron the fabric to be bonded to eliminate wrinkles.
• To bond fabrics, set a dry iron on "cotton."
• When considering fabric choices, remember there are three combinations you could use.
　1. Wrong sides together.
　2. Right side to wrong side.
　3. Two different fabrics.
• Cut two pieces of fabric and one piece of HeatnBond UltraHold the exact same size. If the fabric is cut larger than the bonding material, the edges will not be bonded. If the bonding material is larger than the fabric, you will have a mess on your ironing board.
• Bond a large piece of fabric in sections to be sure each area is fused.
• A dryer sheet is helpful for removing excess glue from your iron.

Appli-bond pieces

Cut two pieces of each fabric to be bonded and one of the bonding material, according to the individual flower instructions.

Following the manufacturer's directions, apply the bonding material to the wrong side of one of the two pieces of fabric. To keep the fabric from slipping during bonding, secure the bonding material to the fabric by placing the iron on several sections of the fabric for one or two seconds. To complete the bonding, move the iron in circles to prevent scorching the fabric or leaving vent marks from the iron. The manufacturer says to use a dry iron for one to two seconds, but in my experience, it is best to press for eight seconds. Use a cloth to protect your ironing surface.

Let the piece cool before you remove the paper backing. For easy paper removal, score the paper with a pin and fold along the scored line, then peel off the paper. After the paper has been removed, bond the two fabric pieces, wrong sides together.

Using a template, draw the desired number of motifs on the bonded fabrics. I like to draw the motifs after the fabrics have been bonded to ensure that the edges adhere when the motifs are cut out. You can draw on the bonded fabrics with a mechanical pencil or a fine-line pen. Be sure to turn your templates over for mirror-image motifs. Cut on the drawn line, leaving no allowances.

Attach motifs according to the instructions given in the patterns. When attaching the petals, overlap them

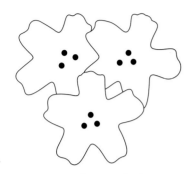

Fig. 1–1. Overlap petals for a more realistic look.

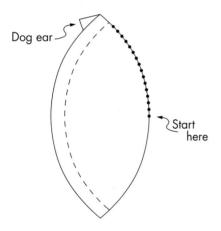

Fig. 1–2. At a point, fold the allowance under and trim off the dog ear.

slightly (Fig. 1–1). If you knot the thread after each motif has been attached, you will be able to reposition individual motifs if you are not satisfied with the arrangement.

Do not drag the thread from one petal to another because you can cause puckering. The use of a finger cot, available in pharmacies, or rubber finger tips, available in office supply stores, will assist you in pulling the needle through the bonded material. It is difficult to embroider through these bonded pieces, so embellishing can be done with a fabric pen.

Curled petals and leaves

Petals should be curled after the flower has been constructed, unless otherwise instructed, to enable you to place the curls more accurately. Be sure to remove the blue, water-soluble pen lines from the fabric before curling the bonded pieces because heat can set the ink.

To curl a bonded piece, heat it with an iron and wrap it around an object to create the desired shape. The small handle of an artist's paintbrush will give you a tight curl. Shape it over your finger for a more gentle curl. Be careful. It will be hot. Crimped edges can be achieved by squeezing the

edges together. Hold the piece in place until it is cool. If you are unhappy with the shape after curling, iron it flat and re-curl it.

"Fluffing" is not a very technical term, but it describes how many of the flowers, such as the Forget-me-nots on page 58, are curled. To fluff, simply place the iron on the completed blossoms and heat for two to three seconds. Then rub your hand back and forth over the blossoms thus fluffing the petals. This technique really adds to the dimension of the flower.

NEEDLE-TURN APPLIQUÉ

Many of the flowers are made with a combination of Appli-bond and traditional appliqué. There are many different methods for turning under the edges of appliqué pieces, including the use of freezer-paper, basted edges, and finger pressing. I prefer needle-turning because it requires less preparation time than these other methods, and with a little practice, it is quite easy if taken a step at a time. Use the appliqué method you like best, but because needle-turning is my method of choice, I will review a few steps that may be helpful if you are unfamiliar with the technique and want to try it.

Trace the templates on the right side of the fabric. Cut the piece to be appliquéd, leaving a ¼" turn-under allowance, by eye, as you cut. To minimize fraying, wait to trim your pieces to a ³⁄₁₆" allowance until you are ready to appliqué them in place. The narrower allowance will be easier to turn. Smooth turned edges will come with practice.

Position the piece to be appliquéd. Baste it in place with a single line of large basting stitches through the middle. I prefer thread basting to pinning because the appliqué thread can catch on the pins. Some quilters pin from the wrong side of the background fabric for the same reason, but when I tried it, I jabbed myself frequently.

With the needle-turn method, your needle is your turning tool. Use thread that matches the fabric to be appliquéd, not the background fabric. Cut a piece of thread that is approximately 18" long. Knot the end that was cut from the spool. Begin appliquéing along a straight or gently curved edge, not at a point. Work from the right side of the fabric. Right-handed quilters generally stitch counterclockwise; left-handed quilters usually stitch clockwise.

Be careful to be consistent with your tension and to hold the piece flat. If it is stitched too loosely, it will not be stable but if it is too tightly stitched, it will pucker and become distorted.

Use the tip of the needle to turn under a tiny portion (⅛" to ¼") of the allowance along the marked line. Knot your thread and bury the knot in the allowance fold. Where the needle comes out of the fold, push it through the background fabric only, close to the edge of the appliqué.

Hold the allowance securely in place with the thumbnail of your free hand. Don't be concerned with what is beyond your thumb (future points, curves, etc.). If you work on just a tiny segment at a time, it will all fall into place.

Guide the needle under the background fabric approximately ¹⁄₁₆" away and bring it up through the folded edge, catching just one or two threads in the fold. Push the needle back into the background fabric, opposite the hole it came out, and just under the fold. Advance your thumb just a tiny bit at a time, needle-turning as you go, until the piece has been completely appliquéd to the background.

Leave unturned any portion of the allowance along an edge that will be covered by another needle-turned appliqué. The unturned edge will decrease bulk, and the appliqué will lie flatter. However, if the piece will be covered by Appli-bond appliqué, you will need to turn under all the edges because the Appli-bond pieces are three-dimensional, and the edges will show. To tie off the stitching, bring your thread to the wrong side and make a knot. Do not cut the background fabric away from the appliqué because this will weaken it.

Points

Stitch up to a point rather than beginning at a point. Take smaller stitches as you approach it. Bring the needle out exactly at the point. Fold the turn-under allowance and trim off the "dog ear" (Fig. 1–2).

With a sweeping motion of the needle, tuck the rest of the allowance under the appliqué. Hold the point in place with your thumb, tug on the thread to make sure the point is sharp. Take a tiny stitch in the tip of the point and in the background fabric to secure the point and elongate it. Continue appliquéing around the piece by using the point of your needle to turn under the edge.

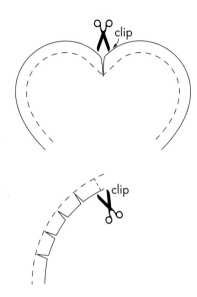

Fig. 1–3. For inside curves and V's, make small clips in the allowance.

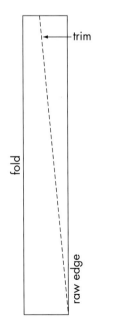

Fig. 1–4. To vary the stem width, sew at an angle.

Inside curves

When appliquéing inside curves and V's, make small clips in the turn-under allowance so it will lie flat. Clip to within one or two threads of the marked line (Fig. 1–3). To reduce fraying, do not clip the curve until you are ready to appliqué the piece.

Bias-strip stems

Use contrasting fabrics for the stems to distinguish them from the leaves and the background. Most of the stems in the patterns were made with ¾"- or 1"-wide bias strips. Narrower stems can be achieved by simply decreasing the width of the strip. If the blossoms are made with the Appli-bond technique, be sure to attach a blossom directly to the end of the stem because the 3-D blossoms will lift up, and the raw edge of the stem will show. True bias is not necessary for most stems. If the curve is gentle, cut it only slightly off-grain.

Stems are cut four times the desired finished width. To construct a stem, cut a strip according to the flower pattern instructions. Fold the strip in half lengthwise, wrong sides together. Do not iron the fold because it will cause a sharp crease, and your stem will not look rounded.

Place the folded strip so that the raw edge just covers the stem placement line on the background fabric. With a small running stitch and matching thread, attach the stem to the background by stitching down the center of the folded stem. It is important that these stitches be small.

The distance you sew from the folded edge determines the finished width of the stem. To vary the width of a stem from wide to narrow, angle your stitching line (Fig. 1–4).

Trim the raw edges close to the stitching line as shown in Figure 1–5. You can then turn the stem over the stitching, covering the raw edge, and appliqué the folded edge in place.

Be sure to appliqué first those stems that branch out from other stems because you will want to cover the unfinished edges.

If a stem is curved, position the folded bias strip on the inside of the curved placement line. Sew the stem in place, trim the raw edge, turn and stretch the stem to the outside of the curve, then appliqué the folded edge of the stem.

If a finished edge is needed on one end, fold in ¼" of the end before folding the strip in half lengthwise.

Make sure you have extended the stem under the bonded petals so that no raw edge will show if the petals are lifted.

MACHINE PIECING

Here are a few tips for machine piecing:

• Accuracy is important to the success of your project.
• The solid line is the cutting line. The dashed line is the stitching line.
• An "r" means reverse the image by turning the template over.
• All cutting instructions include a ¼" seam allowance. Check to make sure that it is an accurate ¼".
• Set your machine at 12 stitches per inch.
• Unless otherwise noted, backstitching is not necessary. Start and stop at the cut edges of the pieces.
• Press the seam allowances toward the darker fabric.

Strip piecing

Some patches can be more easily made by sewing strips together, then cutting the sewn strips in sections. This technique is helpful, especially in patterns such as the Double Irish Chain (page 61) for which the squares can be strip pieced. Make sure that your strips are placed in the proper sequence. Sew the strips in pairs and press the seam allowances toward the darker fabric, then cut to desired size.

Chain sewing

Chain sewing saves time and thread, so you will want to use this technique whenever possible. At the end of a seam, leave the presser foot down. Do not cut the thread. Feed the next pair of patches under the presser foot, close to the first pair, and continue sewing. Continue adding pairs in this manner. After all pairs have been sewn, clip the threads between the pieces to separate them (Fig. 1–6).

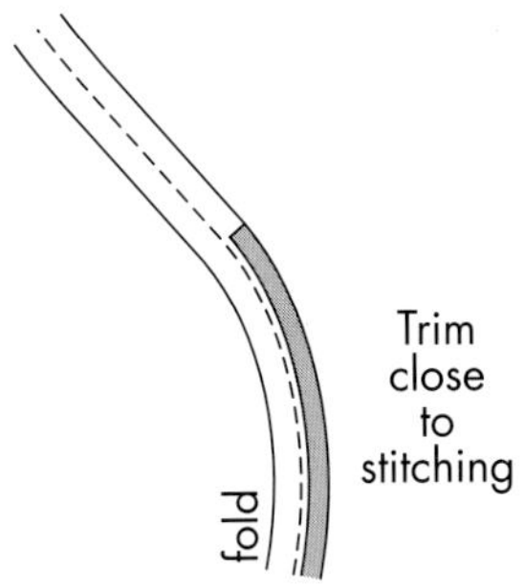

Fig. 1–5. Trim the allowance close to the stitching line.

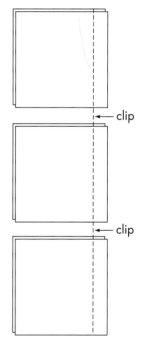

Fig. 1–6. Chain sewing.

ACCURATE SEAM ALLOWANCES

To mark your sewing machine for an accurate ¼" seam allowance, place a ruler under your presser foot and slowly lower the needle, aligning it with the ¼" mark on the ruler. Lower the presser foot. Check to see where the right edge of your presser foot lies. If it is ¼" away from the needle, you can use the edge of the foot as a seam guide. Otherwise, place a piece of masking tape on the throat plate, along the edge of the ruler, and use the tape as a guide.

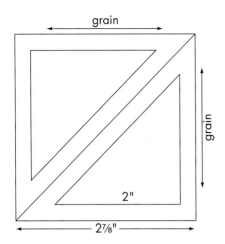

Fig. 1–7. Determining fabric square size for half-square triangles.

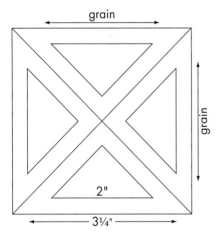

Fig. 1–8. Determining fabric square size for quarter-square triangles.

Half-square triangles

Half-square triangles are some of the most frequently used shapes in a pieced quilt. Quite literally, a half-square triangle is half of a square that has been cut diagonally corner to corner. When a triangle is cut this way, the two short sides are on the straight of grain, and the long side is on the bias.

There is a simple formula to help you determine the size of the square you will need to produce two triangles of a certain finished size. Simply add $7/8$" for seam allowances to the finished size of the triangle (Fig. 1–7). For example, if the finished triangle is 2" on the two short sides, add $7/8$" to the measurement and cut a square $2\frac{7}{8}$".

Quarter-square triangles

Another commonly used patch is the quarter-square triangle. As the name implies, it is one-fourth of a square that has been cut diagonally twice. In this triangle, the long side is on the straight of grain. To find the fabric square size, add $1\frac{1}{4}$" to the finished long side of the triangle. For example, if the long side of the required triangle is 2", add $1\frac{1}{4}$" and cut a square $3\frac{1}{4}$" (Fig. 1–8). These triangles are used whenever you need the straight of grain

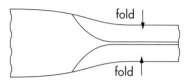

Fig. 1–9 (back of strip). Fold the strip, wrong sides together, with the raw edges butted together.

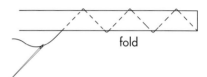

Fig. 1-10. Make a knot in the lower-right corner and sew with a running stitch (front of strip).

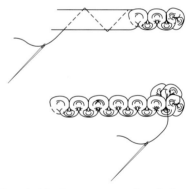

Fig. 1–11. Form rings and tack them in place.

Fig. 1–12. Compare the size of the finished circle to the guide for your project.

on the long edge of a triangle. They are most frequently used when you are setting quilt blocks on the diagonal.

DIMENSIONAL TECHNIQUES

Ruching

Ruching creates a textured look, which is attractive for the center of some flowers.

• Cut a strip on the straight of grain, according to the dimensions in the pattern.

• Fold the strip wrong sides together, with the raw edges butted together (Fig. 1–9).

• Press to hold the folds in place. There is no need to baste.

• Select a quilting thread to match the color of your fabric. Turn the strip over with the folded edges toward you. Make a knot in the lower right corner. Sew a small running stitch across the strip at a 45-degree angle.

• Wrap the thread over the top fold to the opposite side and sew across the strip, to the bottom, at a 45-degree angle. Be sure to always wrap the thread over the folded edge (Fig. 1–10).

• Continue stitching in this manner, gathering the strip frequently to prevent knotting, until you reach the end of the strip.

• Gather the strip tightly and knot the thread, but do not cut it.

• Beginning at the thread end, form a small tight ring and tack it in place with the attached thread (Fig. 1–11).

• Other rings are formed behind the first ring.

• Tack as you go until you reach the end of the strip. Tack the end behind the ruched circle.

• The finished circle should be approximately the size of the guide for the chosen project (Fig. 1–12).

• Using a matching thread, stab-stitch the center of each ruched "petal" to the background fabric.

Rolled buds

• To create a rolled bud, cut a strip of fabric 1½" x 4". Fold it in half lengthwise, wrong sides together, then fold in half crosswise, but slightly off center (Fig. 1–13).

• Hold onto the folded corner, wrap the ends around and spiral downward so that both folded edges show (Fig. 1–14).

• Wrap the bottom edge tightly with thread and knot the thread (Fig. 1–15).

• Appliqué the bud to the background only halfway up the sides so that the top of the bud is free and stands away from the background.

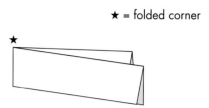

★ = folded corner

Fig. 1–13. Refold the strip in half crosswise, but slightly off center.

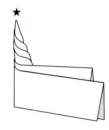

Fig. 1–14. Hold the folded corner and make a spiral with both folded edges showing.

Fig. 1–15. Wrap the bottom tightly with thread.

Fig. 1–16. Fold the circle in half.

Fig. 1–17. Fold in both sides, leaving ¼" unfolded at the top.

Fig. 1–18. Wrap the base with thread.

Folded buds

Folded buds, as used in the Christmas Cactus on page 96, are very attractive.
• Cut a circle according to the pattern instructions.
• Fold the circle in half, wrong sides together (Fig. 1–16).
• Fold in one-third of each side leaving about ¼" unfolded along the top edge (Fig. 1–17).
• Stab-stitch the folds in place along the base.

Double-folded stamens

Double-folded stamens can be used in the center of the Appli-bond flowers that are curled.
• Use a template to cut the circle.
• Fold as directed for the folded buds.
• Repeat the folds, each side again, creating a double fold.
• Wrap the base with thread to hold it in place (Fig. 1–18).
• Tack in place at the base.

EMBROIDERY STITCHES

Embroidery stitches bring appliquéd flowers to life. Sometimes, a contrasting floss color adds interest. It is helpful if you separate the individual strands of the floss and then reassemble them before threading your needle, giving the floss a fuller appearance.

Stab stitch

The stab stitch is used to attach bonded pieces and ruched flowers to the background. Bring the needle straight up through the fabric and pull the thread all the way through to the right side. Push the needle down through the fabric, a stitch length away, and pull the needle and thread all the way through to the back (Fig. 1–19).

Stem stitch

This stitch is used to embroider stems and leaf veins. Use the number of strands of embroidery floss indicated in the pattern directions. This stitch is usually worked from left to right. Bring the needle up through the fabric, then down a stitch length away. Bring the needle to the top again in the middle of the previous stitch and pull the thread all the way through (Fig. 1–20).

French knot

Many of the Appli-bond petals are attached with French knots, allowing the petals to remain free for a 3-D effect. Use the number of strands of embroidery floss indicated.

To make a French knot, bring the needle up through the bonded fabric where you want the knot. Wrap the thread around the needle the suggested number of times. Holding the thread taut, push the needle straight down through the fabric, close to where the thread first emerged but not in the same hole. Hold the wraps in place and pull the needle and thread completely through the fabric and the thread wraps. Do not pull the thread too tight, which would diminish the size of the knot (Fig. 1–21).

Embroider the suggested number of knots in each blossom. When attaching multiple blossoms, it is not necessary to make an ending knot after each French knot. However, you should knot and cut the thread after each blossom has been attached. Dragging the thread from one blossom to another may cause the piece to pucker.

Lazy-daisy stitch

The lazy daisy gives a lacy effect as seen on the California poppy buds on page 50. Bring the needle up through the fabric. Push the needle down as close to where the thread first emerged as possible, but not in the same hole. As you pull the thread through, leave a small loop. Bring the needle up through the loop, and make a small anchor stitch over the loop (Fig. 1–23).

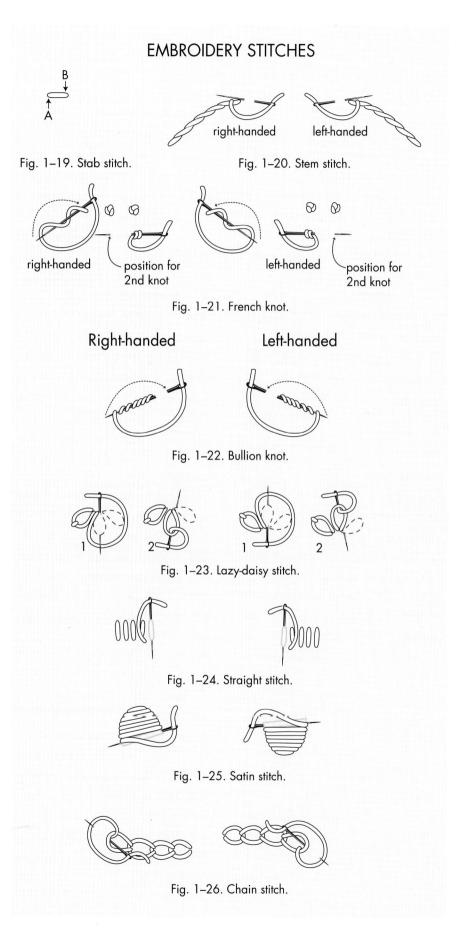

EMBROIDERY STITCHES

Fig. 1–19. Stab stitch.

right-handed   left-handed

Fig. 1–20. Stem stitch.

right-handed   position for 2nd knot   left-handed   position for 2nd knot

Fig. 1–21. French knot.

Right-handed   Left-handed

Fig. 1–22. Bullion knot.

1   2   1   2

Fig. 1–23. Lazy-daisy stitch.

Fig. 1–24. Straight stitch.

Fig. 1–25. Satin stitch.

Fig. 1–26. Chain stitch.

Straight stitch

Bring the needle up through the fabric. Push it back down at the desired distance (Fig. 1–24, page 19). You can use a single straight stitch or several stitches together to achieve the desired effect. Vary the length and direction to add interest. The straight stitch is used on the Violets on page 90.

Satin stitch

Mark the desired shape on the fabric. Using the number of floss strands suggested in the pattern, fill in the shape with straight stitches sewn close together (Fig. 1–25, page 19).

Chain stitch

The chain stitch makes an interesting stem. (See the violet on page 91.) Bring the needle up through the fabric and make a loop with the floss. Go down as close to where the thread emerged as possible, but not into the hole. Bring the needle out a stitch length away and bring the tip of the needle over the thread. Repeat to make a chain (Fig. 1–26, page 19).

QUILTING

Marking

The quilting design can be marked on the quilt top before the quilt is layered. I find this method much easier

and more accurate than marking a layered quilt. Mark the design with a blue water-soluble pen or a light pencil (#3 or #4). Chalk pencils and saral paper (described on page 10) show well on dark fabrics. Test to see that all the markings can be removed without damaging your fabric.

Before marking the top, press it well. Lay it on a flat surface so that marking will be easier and more accurate. Mark lightly. Some quilting patterns do not require marking, such as quilting in the ditch, outline quilting, or echo quilting. These patterns can be done "by eye." Do not press the top after marking it because the heat will set the marks.

Grid lines can be marked with a pencil and ruler or masking tape. It's best not to leave the tape on your quilt for an extended period of time because it may leave a residue that can damage your fabric.

Quilting designs

Quilting adds to the overall design and brings the quilt to life. Plan the quilting carefully to complement the appliqué patterns. Geometric quilting, simple grids, cross-hatching, or a series of straight lines provide contrast to the many curves in the flowers.

The following two quilting patterns, traditionally used for appliqué quilts, easily lend themselves to either hand or machine quilting.

OUTLINE STITCHING. This pattern follows the outlines of the appliquéd pieces, generally about 1/8" away from them. It is not necessary to outline each appliquéd piece. Outline quilting is generally done before any background quilting and does not require marking. Just eyeball it.

BACKGROUND QUILTING. This term refers to quilting patterns, such as grids or stipple quilting, that compress the background, allowing the appliqué to stand out in relief. Traditionally, quilting lines are stitched up to the appliquéd pieces, but not through them. However, with Appli-bond, it is important to quilt not only up to but also under the 3-D pieces to force them to stand free of the background.

FINISHING TOUCHES
Backing

The backing should measure 4" longer and wider than the quilt top. If the quilt measures less than 38" on one edge, you will not need to piece the backing. If the quilt top is larger than 38", you will need to piece it. Determine whether it is more economical to piece the backing horizontally or vertically (Fig. 2–27). Sew the panels together (minus selvages) and press the seam allowances open.

You can add extra interest to your quilt with a creative backing. You may want to carry the flower theme to the back of the quilt with a matching flower-patterned fabric or include a few of the pieced blocks.

Layering

Unfold the batting and allow time for the creases to relax. Placing it in a dryer on air-fluff often helps. To layer the quilt pieces, lay the backing, wrong side up, on a flat surface. Center the batting on the backing. Then center the pieced top, right side up, on the batting. When making a wallhanging, I prefer using a low-loft batting.

Basting is an important step for Appli-bond appliqué quilts because you will probably not be using a hoop for quilting because the 3-D elements can get in the way of the hoop. The more basting you do, the less chance there is for shifting and puckering. Baste from the center out, in all directions, at 3" intervals. If you intend to hand quilt, thread basting is advisable. If you plan to machine quilt,

pinning is recommended. Baste along the outside edges, too, to prevent the quilt from slipping and stretching while you apply the binding. Remove the basting as each area is quilted. This way, you are more apt to remove all of it, and it is much easier to examine a small area for missed threads than a whole quilt.

Double-fold binding

You may be anxious to finish your project so you can start the next one, but it's best not rush. Taking shortcuts at this point can undermine all the effort you have put into the quilt.

Trim the excess batting and backing from the quilt top. To make sure that the corners are square, check each corner with a large square ruler (12" to 16"). Trim the corners as needed to square them. For a double-fold binding, I cut my fabric strips 2" wide, but widths up to 2½" can be used with this binding method.

Place two strips, right sides together, at a 45-degree angle and sew them together as shown in Fig. 1–28. Trim the seam allowances to ¼" and press them open. Continue to add strips until you have the desired length, which is the perimeter of the quilt plus at least 6".

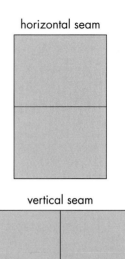

horizontal seam

vertical seam

Fig. 1–27. The backing can be pieced horizontally or vertically.

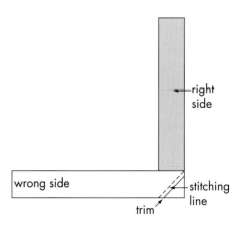

right side

wrong side

stitching line

trim

Fig. 1–28. Sew strips together at a 45-degree angle.

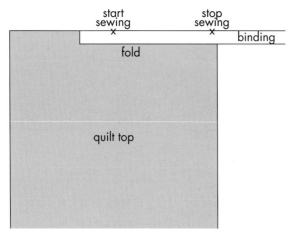

Fig. 1–29. Stop sewing ¼" from the corner.

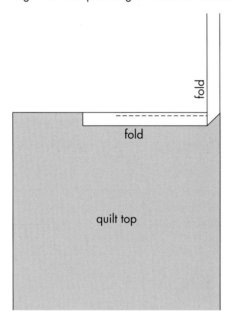

Fig. 1–30. Fold the binding straight up.

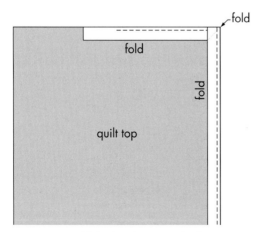

Fig. 1–31. Fold the binding straight down, aligning it with the quilt's raw edge.

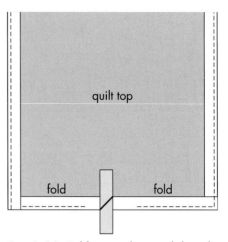

Fig. 1–32. Fold one tail up and the other down at 45-degree angles.

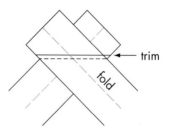

Fig. 1–33. Sew the ends together along the creases.

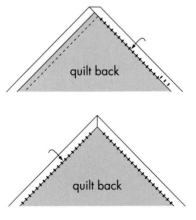

Fig. 1–34. On the back of the quilt, fold in one side of the binding and then the other to create a miter.

Fold the binding in half wrong sides together. Start in the center of one side of the quilt and pin the raw edges of the binding to the raw edges of the quilt.

Start sewing approximately 6" from the end of the binding strip (Fig. 1–29). Sew ¼" from the raw edge and stop stitching ¼" from the corner. Backstitch, clip the threads, and remove the quilt from the presser foot.

Fold the binding up and away from the quilt top, creating a right angle (Fig. 1–30).

Next, fold the binding down (Fig. 1–31). Be sure to align the raw edges of the binding with the raw edges of the quilt on the second side. Starting at the folded edge, continue stitching with a ¼" seam allowance.

Repeat these instructions for all four corners.

Stop stitching the binding to the quilt approximately 8" from where you began. Pin the binding in place. Turn and press one tail of the binding up at a 45-degree angle and other tail down at a 45-degree angle, as shown in Fig. 1–32. Press the folds well to mark the seam line.

Unpin the binding from the quilt and pin the strips together with the pressed folded lines together and sew them along the crease (Fig. 1–33). Trim the seam allowances to ¼" and press them open. Pin the binding to the quilt and finish sewing it in place.

Press the binding away from the quilt. Fold the binding to the back and blind stitch it to the backing. Make sure that the binding at the corners is folded to form a miter on the back, like the one on the front (Fig. 1–34).

Finishing

The final stitches are the best. Remove all visible markings. Be sure to label your quilt. Family members, friends, and collectors will thank you. Include on your label your name, the date the quilt was completed, the town and state where the quilt was made, and any pertinent information about what makes the quilt unique.

Chapter 2
PATTERNS

Water Lily
LADY OF THE LAKE

Pieced and appliquéd by the author; quilted by Jackie Davis.

Water Lily
LADY OF THE LAKE
traditional block

LADY OF THE LAKE

Finished quilt: 25" x 25"
Finished block: 12½" x 12½"
Number of blocks: 4

FABRIC REQUIREMENTS

The yardage is based on fabric at least 42" wide. You may want to buy a little extra if you like to make sample blocks or if you want a margin for error in rotary cutting.

Fabric	Yards
Green	⅛
White	⅜
Blue	⅜
Sky	⅜
Water	⅜
Backing	⅞
Binding	¼
Batting	29" x 29"

PREPARATION

Cut strips from selvage to selvage.

GREEN. Cut one strip 3⅜", then cut four 3⅜" squares from the strip. Cut squares in half diagonally to make eight half-square triangles.

WHITE. Cut three strips 3⅜". Layer the strips, both right side up, and cut 32 – 3⅜" squares. Cut the squares in half diagonally to make 64 half-square triangles.

BLUE. Cut three strips 3⅜". Layer the strips, right side up, and cut 28 squares, 3⅜". Cut the squares in half diagonally to make 56 half-square triangles.

SKY AND WATER. From each fabric, cut one strip 8⅜", then cut two 8⅜" squares from each strip. Cut the squares in half diagonally to make four sky and four water half-square triangles.

CONSTRUCTION

Carefully note the placement of all smaller half-square triangles. Each block is different.

• Sew four sky triangles and four water triangles together to make four squares 8" x 8".

• Sew eight green triangles to eight white triangles to make eight squares 3" x 3".

• Sew the remaining 56 white triangles to 56 blue triangles to make 56 squares 3" x 3".

• Sew three blue and white squares together (Fig. 2–1). Make eight of these three-square units.

three-square unit

Fig. 2–1.

• Sew four blue and white squares together (Fig. 2–2). Make eight four-square units.

four-square unit

Fig. 2–2.

• Sew three-square units to top and bottom of each sky and water square (Fig. 2–3).

Fig. 2–3.

• Divide the eight four-square units into two piles. Sew one green-and-white square to one end of each unit in one pile and to the opposite end of each unit in the other pile.

• Sew these five-square units to the remaining sides of the blocks (Fig. 2–4).

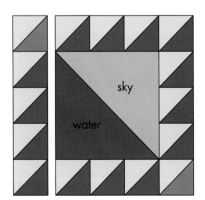

Fig. 2–4.

• Before joining the blocks to complete the quilt top, appli-que a Water Lily (page 27) to each block.

• Join the blocks to complete the quilt top (see quilt assembly diagram).

• Layer the backing, batting, and quilt top. Baste the layers and quilt them.

• Cut three 2½" strips. Sew them together with a diagonal seam to make continuous, double-fold binding. Bind the raw edges to finish the quilt.

At a Glance

Machine piecing, p. 15
Backing, p. 20
Layering, p. 21
Quilting ideas, p. 20
Binding, p. 21

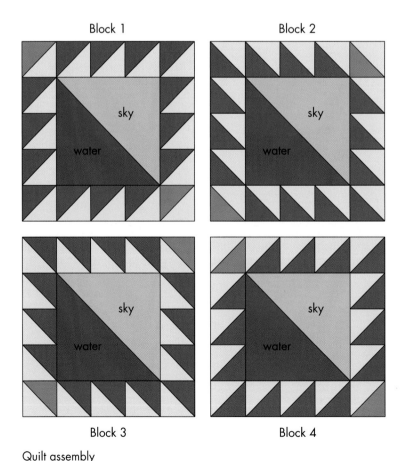

Block 1

Block 2

Block 3

Block 4

Quilt assembly

Water Lily
LADY OF THE LAKE
Appli-bond appliqué

WATER LILY

Number of flowers: 4
Flower fits in an 8" x 8" space.

SUPPLIES
HeatnBond UltraHold: ⅔ yd.
Embroidery floss: yellow

TEMPLATES
Small petal
Medium petal
Large petal
Leaf

FABRIC REQUIREMENTS

Fabric	Yards
Petals	⅓
Leaves	⅛

PREPARATION
Appli-bond appliqué:

PETALS. Cut two fabric pieces and one bonding piece 20" x 11".

LEAVES. Cut two fabric pieces and one bonding piece 4½" x 16".

Bond the two petal pieces and the two leaf pieces. Trace the templates on the bonded fabrics and cut 16 small, 24 medium, and 32 large petals, and four leaves.

Use your iron to heat each bonded petal for one to two seconds and gently curl it by shaping the petal over your index finger.

CONSTRUCTION
• Use a blue water-soluble pen to trace the outline of the Water Lily pattern on a completed Lady of the Lake block.
• Use two strands of embroidery floss in your Appli-bond needle and stem stitch to attach the bonded leaf to the block by embroidering the veins.
• Use matching thread and stab stitches to attach the petals to the background, starting with the large petals and progressing to the small ones.
• Embroider the center with approximately 15 French knots. Use two strands of yellow embroidery floss and wrap the needle three times for each knot.
• Create the stamens with three free-form bullion knots.
• Erase the blue lines with a cotton swab and cold water.
• Continue with the quilt-making instructions for the LADY OF THE LAKE quilt on page 26.

center seam

3 lg.

4 lg.

2 lg.

3 med.

2 med.

1 sm.

4 med.

5 lg.

2 sm.

1 lg.

6 lg.

1 med.

4 sm.

3 sm.

5 med.

7 lg.

6 med.

8 lg.

leaf

center seam

Shaded pieces indicate Appli-bond

Petal Play THE TRADITIONAL WAY — *Joan Shay*

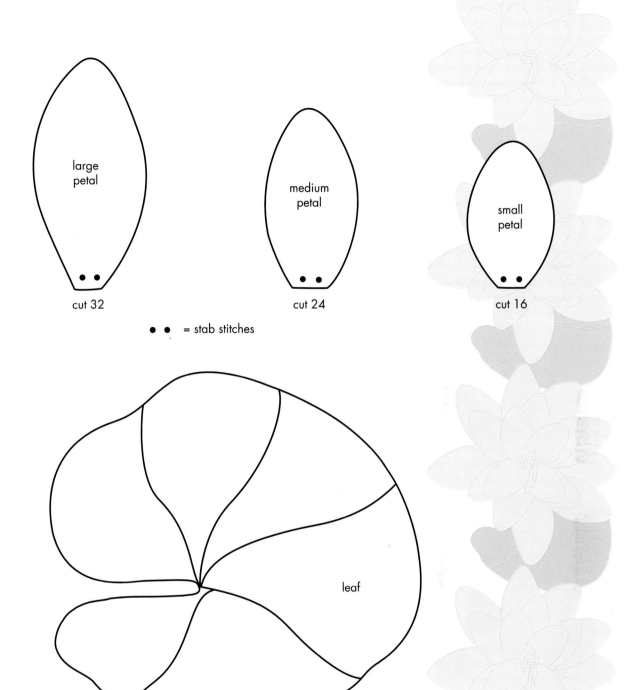

large
petal

cut 32

medium
petal

cut 24

small
petal

cut 16

● ● = stab stitches

leaf

cut 4

At a Glance

Templates, p. 10
Appli-bond appliqué, p. 11
Curled petals and leaves, p. 12
Embroidery stitches, p. 18

Magnolia
DOUBLE WEDDING RING

Made by the author.

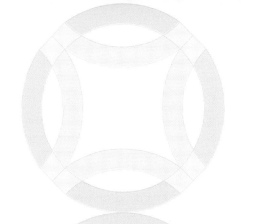

Magnolia
DOUBLE WEDDING RING
traditional block

DOUBLE WEDDING RING

Finished quilt: 26¾" x 26¾"
Finished block: 15¾" x 15¾"
Number of blocks: 4

TEMPLATES

Background
Melon
Arc
Connector

FABRIC REQUIREMENTS

The yardage is based on fabric at least 42" wide. You may want to buy a little extra if you like to make sample blocks or if you want a margin for error in rotary cutting.

Fabric	Yards
Background	
and melons	⅜
Pink arcs	
and binding	1
Green arcs	½
Connecting pieces	¼
Backing	1
Batting	30" x 30"

PREPARATION

A small rotary cutter is recommended for cutting curved pieces. If you would rather purchase acrylic Wedding Ring templates, information can be found under Home Shopping on page 109.

BACKGROUND. Use the background template to cut four pieces. Fold each piece in half in both directions to find the center of each side. Mark the centers in the seam allowances with a notch, pin, or pencil dot (Fig. 2–5). If you notch the centers, be careful not to cut into the seam line.

MELONS. Use the melon template to cut 12 pieces. Mark the centers of both sides (Fig. 2–6). Place a dot at each point where the seam lines cross (Fig. 2–7).

ARCS. Use the arc template to cut 12 pink pieces and 12 green pieces. Mark the centers (Fig. 2–8).

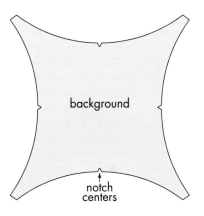

Fig. 2–5.

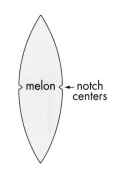

Fig. 2–6.

Fig. 2–7.

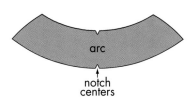

Fig. 2–8.

Fig. 2–9.

Fig. 2–10.

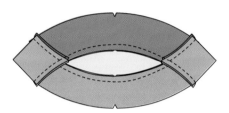

Fig. 2–11.

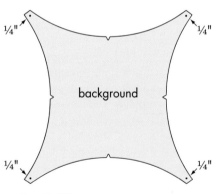

Fig. 2–12.

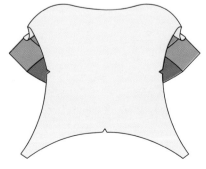

Fig. 2–13.

CONNECTOR. Use connector template to make 24 pieces, cut on the straight of grain or on the bias, but bias is recommended.

CONSTRUCTION

When joining melons and arcs, press seam allowances toward the arcs. When sewing the melon units to the background pieces, press seam allowances toward the background.

• With right sides together, sew a connector to each end of 12 arcs, six of each color (Fig. 2–9). Sew with the connector on top. Be careful not to stretch the bias.

• Matching centers, sew the remaining arcs to melons, right sides together (Fig. 2–10).

• Sew the arc/connector units to the melons, aligning the seams of the connectors to the dots on the melons. Sew with the arcs on top (Fig. 2–11).

• With a pencil, mark a dot on all four tails of each background piece where the seam lines cross (Fig. 2–12).

• Place all the pieces on a flat surface to check the proper color placement.

• Align the melon units with the background pieces. Pin through the center of the arc and the background piece. Also pin the connecting corners at the marked points on the background pieces.

• Sew, right sides together, with the background piece on top (Fig. 2–13). Stop and start at the points. Do not join the connectors yet.

• Check the color placement as you add the melon units to the background pieces. Sew four melon units to one background piece (Fig. 2–14), three melon units to two background pieces (Fig. 2–15), and two melon units to the remaining background piece (Fig. 2–16).

• Join the full circle to one three-sided unit (Fig. 2–17). Do not join the connectors yet.

• Join the remaining three-sided unit to the two-sided piece (Fig. 2–18).

• To join the two rows of rings, match the centers of the melons to the centers of the background pieces (Fig. 2–19). Sew with the background pieces on top. Do not join the connectors yet.

• To complete the top, align the connectors, right sides together, and sew.

• Construct a Magnolia flower (page 36) in the center of each Wedding Ring.

• Layer the backing, batting, and quilt top. Baste the layers and quilt them.

• For the binding, cut three 2½" strips. Sew them together, end to end with a diagonal seam, to make continuous, double-fold binding. Bind the raw edges to finish the quilt.

At a Glance

Machine piecing, p. 15
Backing, p. 20
Layering, p. 21
Quilting ideas, p. 20
Binding, p. 21

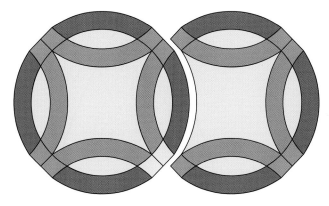

Fig. 2–17.

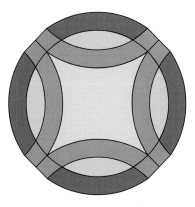

Fig. 2–14. Sew one of these.

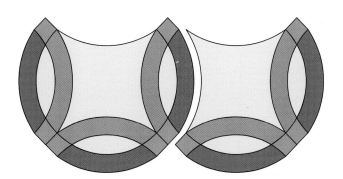

Fig. 2–18.

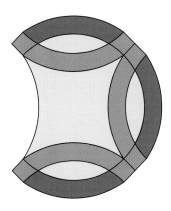

Fig. 2–15. Sew two of these.

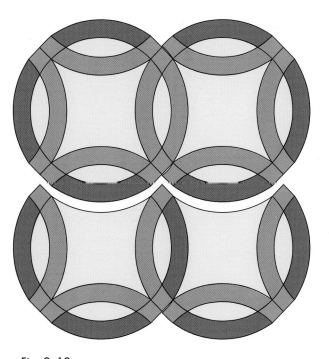

Fig. 2–19.

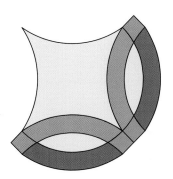

Fig. 2–16. Sew one of these.

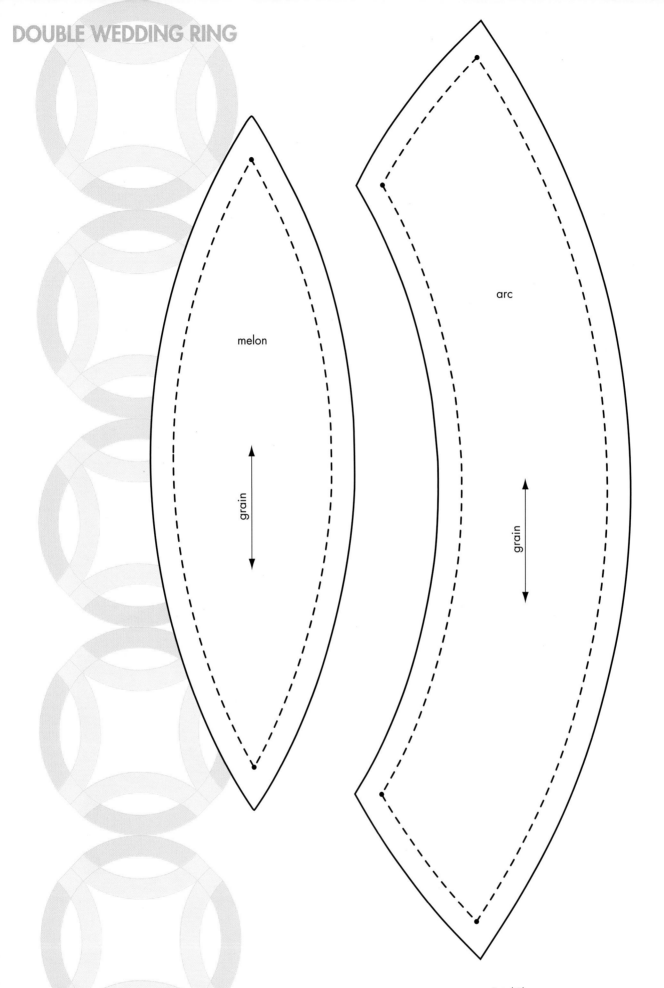

melon

grain

arc

grain

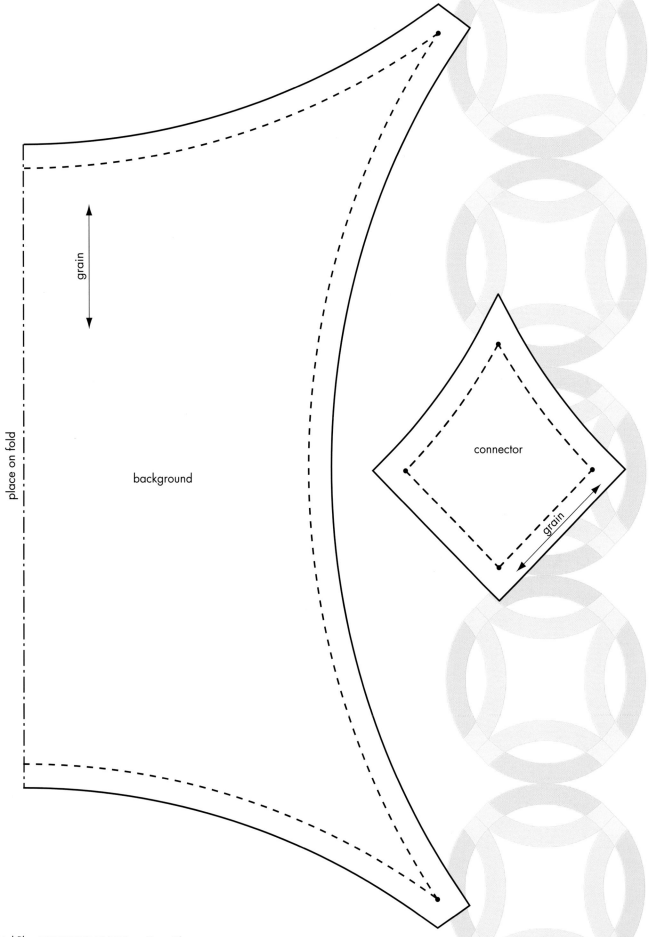

grain

place on fold

background

connector

grain

Magnolia
DOUBLE WEDDING RING
Appli-bond appliqué

MAGNOLIA

Number of flowers: 4
Flower fits in an 8" x 8" space.

SUPPLIES
HeatnBond UltraHold: ¾ yd.
Embroidery floss: green, yellow, and pink

TEMPLATES
Blossom
Leaves 1–6

FABRIC REQUIREMENTS

Fabric	Yards
Blossoms	¼
Leaves	⅓

PREPARATION
Appli-bond appliqué:

BLOSSOMS. Cut two fabric pieces and one bonding piece 5" x 20".

Bond the two blossom fabric pieces. Use the blossom template (shaded flower on page 37) to trace four flowers on the bonded fabric. Cut out the flowers.

Traditional appliqué:
BLOSSOMS. Trace the blossom template on the right side of the fabric. Cut four blossoms, adding ³⁄₁₆" allowances.

LEAVES. Trace the leaf templates on the right side of the fabric. Cut four of each leaf, adding a ³⁄₁₆" allowance.

CONSTRUCTION
• In the center of each Wedding Ring, trace the outline of the Magnolia blossom with a blue water-soluble pen.
• Appliqué the leaves to the background and use the stem stitch with two strands of floss to embroider the veins in the leaves.

• Appliqué a blossom over the leaves. The leaves and background are not cut away from under the flower to give it added dimension.
• Use a blue water-soluble pen to draw a circle, about the size of a dime, in the center of a bonded blossom.
• Place the bonded blossom on top of the appliquéd blossom, slightly off center, so the bottom one peeks out.
• With two strands of pink embroidery floss and the Appli-bond needle wrapped three times, outline the center circle with pink French knots. Sew the knots through the bonded blossom, the appliquéd blossom, and the background.
• With two strands of floss and the needle wrapped three times, fill in the pink circle with yellow French knots.
• Use the stem stitch with two strands of pink floss to secure the bonded blossom to the appliquéd blossom along the vein lines.
• Erase the blue lines with a cotton swab and cold water.
• Curl the bonded petals as desired.
• Finish the quilt, following instructions on page 32.

blossom
template

1

2

3

4

5

6

Shaded pieces indicate Appli-bond

1
leaf

2
leaf

3
leaf

4
leaf

5
leaf

6
leaf

At a Glance

Dandelion
HOLE IN THE BARN DOOR

Pieced by Mary Hayes, appliquéd by the author, and quilted by Jackie Davis.

Dandelion
HOLE IN THE BARN DOOR
traditional block

HOLE IN THE BARN DOOR

Finished quilt: 30" x 30"
Finished block: 15"
Number of blocks: 4

FABRIC REQUIREMENTS

The yardage is based on fabric at least 42" wide. You may want to buy a little extra if you like to make sample blocks or if you want a margin for error in rotary cutting.

Fabric	Yards
Black	1
Red	¾
Backing	1
Binding	⅜
Batting	34" x 34"

PREPARATION

Cut strips selvage to selvage.

BLACK. Cut two strips 5⅞", then cut eight 5⅞" squares from the strips. Cut the squares in half diagonally to make 16 half-square triangles.

Cut two 5½" strips. Trim the remainder of the 5⅞" strip to 5½" wide. Cut 16 rectangles 3" x 5½" and four 5½" squares from the three strips.

RED. Cut two strips 5⅞", then cut eight 5⅞" squares from the strips. Cut the squares in half diagonally to make 16 half-square triangles.

Cut two 5½" strips. Trim the remainder of the 5⅞" strip to 5½" wide. Cut 16 rectangles 3" x 5½" from the three strips.

CONSTRUCTION

• Sew 16 black half-square triangles to 16 red half-square triangles to make 16 half-square units (Fig. 2–20). Press seam allowances toward the black fabric.

• Join 16 black rectangles to 16 red rectangles to make 16 double-rectangle units (Fig. 2–21). Press seam allowances toward the black.

• Sew two half-square units to eight of the double-rectangle units (Fig. 2–22).

• Sew two double-rectangle units to each of the four 5½" black center squares (Fig. 2–23).

• Join the three rows to complete each block (Fig. 2–24).

• Before sewing the blocks together, appliqué a dandelion (page 42) in the center of each one.

• Join the blocks as shown in the quilt assembly diagram.

• Layer the backing, batting, and quilt top. Baste the layers and quilt them.

• Cut four 2½" strips. Sew them together, end to end with a diagonal seam, to make continuous, double-fold binding. Bind the raw edges to finish the quilt.

Fig. 2–20.

Fig. 2–21.

Fig. 2–22.

Fig. 2–23.

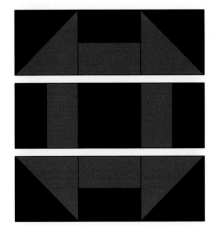

Fig. 2–24.

Quilt assembly

At a Glance

Machine piecing, p. 15
Backing, p. 20
Layering, p. 21
Quilting ideas, p. 20
Binding, p. 21

Dandelion
HOLE IN THE BARN DOOR
Appli-bond appliqué

DANDELION

Number of flowers: 4
Flower fits in a 6" x 8" space.

SUPPLIES
HeatnBond UltraHold: ¼ yd.
Embroidery floss: yellow, brown, and green

TEMPLATES
Blossom circles:
    Center,
    1", 1¼", 1½", 1¾"
Bud
Calyx
Leaves 1–4

FABRIC REQUIREMENTS

Fabric	Yards
Blossoms	¼
Calyx and leaf 2	scraps
Leaves 1r and 4	scraps
Leaves 1 and 3	scraps

PREPARATION

Appli-bond appliqué:
BLOSSOMS. Cut two fabric pieces and one bonding piece 8" x 8".

CALYX AND LEAF 2. Cut two fabric pieces and one bonding piece 2½" x 2½".

LEAVES 1R AND 4. Cut two fabric pieces and one bonding piece 2½" x 3½".

LEAVES 1 AND 3. Cut two fabric pieces and one bonding piece 2½" x 3½".

Bond each pair of fabrics for the blossoms, calyxes, and leaves. Trace the four blossom circle templates (1" – 1¾") on the bonded fabrics and cut four of *each*.

Trace the center circle in the center of each blossom circle with a fine-line mechanical pencil.

Cut each petal as shown in Fig. 2–25, stopping at the marked center circle.

Cut the rest of the circle into petal shapes as shown in Fig. 2–26. Be careful not to cut off any petals.

Trace around the calyx template on the bonded fabric for four calyxes and cut.

Trace the five (including 1r) leaf templates on the bonded fabrics and cut four of each leaf.

Traditional appliqué:
BUDS. Trace the template for four buds on the right side of the fabric.

Cut the four buds, adding a ³⁄₁₆" turn-under allowance by eye as you cut.

STEMS. Cut four bias strips ¾" x 10". Fold the strips in half lengthwise, wrong sides together. Do not press.

FRINGED BLOSSOM CENTER. Cut 16 – 6" pieces of yellow floss. Fold each piece into 1" lengths, creating a figure-eight. Tie the center with a 10" piece of floss (Fig. 2–27).

Cut the folds, being careful not to cut the ties. They will be used to attach the fringed pieces to the blossoms.

CONSTRUCTION

• Trace the outline of the dandelion pattern on the Hole in the Barn Door blocks. Use the dotted square in the pattern as a placement guide.

• Appliqué the stems to the background. Make sure the stems extend under the blossoms, which can be lifted.

• Appliqué the buds to the background. With two strands of floss, wrap the Appli-bond needle two times for each French knot. Use three knots to attach each bonded bud calyx to the background.

• Use two strands of embroidery floss, your Appli-bond needle and the stem stitch to attach the bonded leaves to the background by embroidering along the veins.

• With matching thread, stab-stitch the leaves where indicated to hold them in place.

• Curl the leaves by heating them with an iron and pressing the edges together between your thumb and index finger. Hold until cool.

• Layer one of each size blossom circle on top of each other and join them with a stab stitch through the center.

• To attach a fringed blossom center, thread an Appli-bond

needle with one of the floss center's ties. Place the fringed piece horizontally on the blossom (Fig. 2–28). Stab stitch through the center of the blossom and the background. Repeat with the other tie.

• Tie the two floss pieces together on the back of the block.

• Lay a second fringed blossom center on the blossom vertically and attach it in the same manner (Fig. 2–29). Attach two fringed centers to each blossom and fluff the fringes.

• Embroider the roots using two strands of brown embroidery floss and the stem stitch.

• Use a fine-line fabric pen to draw the vein lines on the bud.

• Heat the blossom petals with an iron and fluff them.

• Curl the leaves by heating them with an iron and gently squeezing them together. Hold until cool.

At a Glance

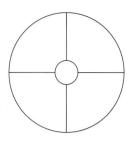

Fig. 2–25.

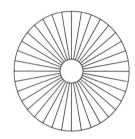

Fig. 2–26.

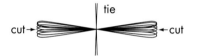

Fig. 2–27.

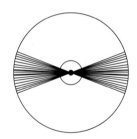

Fig. 2–28.

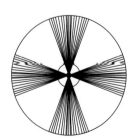

Fig. 2–29.

1r

1

2

3

4

Shaded pieces indicate Appli-bond

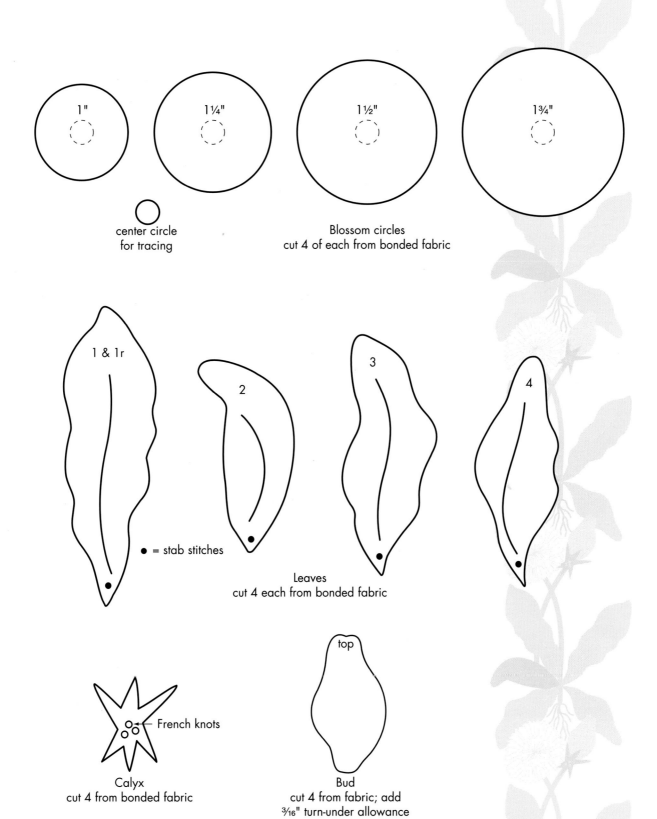

1"

1¼"

1½"

1¾"

center circle
for tracing

Blossom circles
cut 4 of each from bonded fabric

1 & 1r

2

3

4

● = stab stitches

Leaves
cut 4 each from bonded fabric

top

French knots

Calyx
cut 4 from bonded fabric

Bud
cut 4 from fabric; add
³⁄₁₆" turn-under allowance

California Poppy
ROCKY ROAD TO CALIFORNIA
(Drunkard's Path)

Pieced by the author, appliquéd by Adelaide Chandler; quilted by Jackie Davis.

California Poppy
ROCKY ROAD TO CALIFORNIA
(Drunkard's Path)
traditional block

ROCKY ROAD TO CALIFORNIA
(DRUNKARD'S PATH)

Finished quilt: 32" x 32"
Finished block: 4"
Number of blocks: 64

TEMPLATES
Curve A
Curve B

FABRIC REQUIREMENTS
The yardage is based on fabric at least 42" wide. You may want to buy a little extra if you like to make sample blocks or if you want a margin for error in rotary cutting.

Fabric	Yards
Light	1
Dark	1
Backing	1
Binding	⅜
Batting	36" x 36"

PREPARATION
Cut strips selvage to selvage. A small rotary cuter will make cutting curves easier. Information for purchasing curved templates can be found in the Home Shopping (page 109). Please note that seam allowances are included in these template patterns.

Layer the light fabric on the dark fabric. Cut four 4½" strips. You will have four light and four dark strips.

Cut the layered strips into 4½" squares to make 32 light and 32 dark squares.

With light and dark fabrics layered, cut two 6" strips. You will have two light and two dark strips.

Cut the layered 6" strips into 16 light and 16 dark 3½" x 6" rectangles.

Use the Curve A template to cut the corner out of all of the 64 squares (Fig. 2–30). To eliminate confusion, separate the discarded corners and save them for another project.

Use the Curve B template to cut opposite corners from all of the 32 rectangles (Fig. 2-31). You will have 32 light and 32 dark B curves.

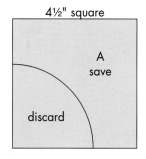

Fig. 2–30.

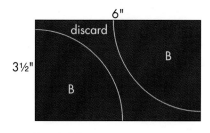

Fig. 2-31.

Fig. 2–32.

Fig. 2–33.

Fig. 2–34.

CONSTRUCTION

• Fold a light A in half and finger press the fold at the curved edge to mark the center. Repeat for a dark B.

• Place the light A and a dark B right sides together. Match and pin the centers. Align the straight edges and the curves and pin at both ends. To eliminate puckering, sew with the flat piece, A, on the bottom (Fig. 2–32).

• Stitch slowly. Use a stiletto or pin to align the curved edges as you sew. Do not stitch more than ½" at a time before you re-align the edges. Press seam allowances toward the darker fabric. Make a total of 64 squares, 32 of each square as shown in Fig. 2–33.

• Sew four squares together to complete a block (Fig. 2–34). Make 16 blocks. Wait to press.

• Arrange the blocks on a flat surface to ensure proper placement. You will need to rotate some of the blocks.

• Sew four blocks together as in Fig. 2–35. Make four rows like this. Two of these rows will be used as row 2; simply turn two rows upside down for quilt assembly (Fig. 2-36).

• Assemble the quilt by rows as shown in the quilt assembly diagram. Press all seam allowances for even-number rows in one direction and in the opposite direction for odd-numbered rows. Join the rows to complete the pieced quilt top.

• Appliqué a California Poppy (page 50) in the four light areas in the quilt center. See quilt assembly diagram and the photo on page 46 for placement.

• Layer the backing, batting, and quilt top. Baste the layers and quilt them.

• Cut four 2½" strips. Sew them together, end to end with a diagonal seam, to make continuous, double-fold binding. Bind the raw edges to finish the quilt.

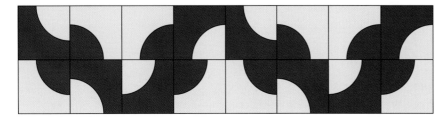

Fig. 2–35. Assemble four-block rows.

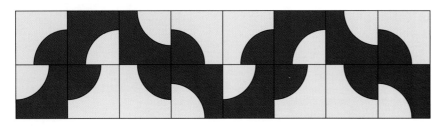

Fig. 2–36. Use two of the four-block rows turned upside down for row 2.

row 1

row 2

row 1

row 2

Quilt assembly. Attach flowers to background areas marked with X.

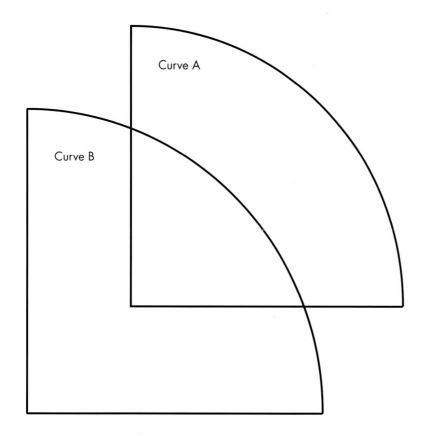

Curve A

Curve B

At a Glance

Machine piecing, p. 15
Backing, p. 20
Layering, p. 21
Quilting ideas, p. 20
Binding, p. 21

California Poppy
ROCKY ROAD TO CALIFORNIA
(Drunkard's Path)
Appli-bond appliqué

CALIFORNIA POPPY

Number of flowers: 4
Flower fits in a 7½" x 7½" space.

SUPPLIES
HeatnBond UltraHold: ¼ yd.
Embroidery floss: green, black, and orange

TEMPLATES
Petal
Bud

FABRIC REQUIREMENTS

Fabric	Yards
Petals, buds	¼
Stems	¼

PREPARATION
Appli-bond appliqué:
PETALS. Cut two fabric pieces and one bonding piece 6" x 12".

Bond the two petal pieces. Trace the petal template on the bonded fabric and cut 32 petals.

Traditional appliqué:
BUDS. Trace the bud template on the right side of the fabric.

Cut four buds, adding ³⁄₁₆" turn-under allowances by eye as you cut.

STEMS. Cut four bias strips ½" x 18".

CONSTRUCTION
• Use a blue water-soluble pen to trace the outline of the California Poppy on the completed ROCKY ROAD TO CALIFORNIA quilt top.
• For the stems, fold the ½" x 18" bias strips in half lengthwise, wrong sides together. Do not press. Appliqué the stems to the background. Make sure the stems extend under the flowers because the petals will lift up.
• Use two strands of floss, your Appli-bond needle, and the stem stitch to embroider the stems. Create the feathery leaves by sewing V shapes.
• Appliqué the bud. Use the stem stitch with one strand of floss to embroider the bud vein. With one strand of embroidery floss, outline the bud with the lazy daisy stitch.

• Attach the petals to the background with stab stitches or basting glue.
• Use two strands of orange floss and the straight stitch to create the center of the flowers as shown in Fig. 2–37.

Fig. 2–37.

• Place four French knots in the center of each flower. Use two strands of black floss and wrap the needle three times.
• Erase the blue lines with a cotton swab and cold water.
• Curl the bottom petal of each flower.

At a Glance

← placement lines

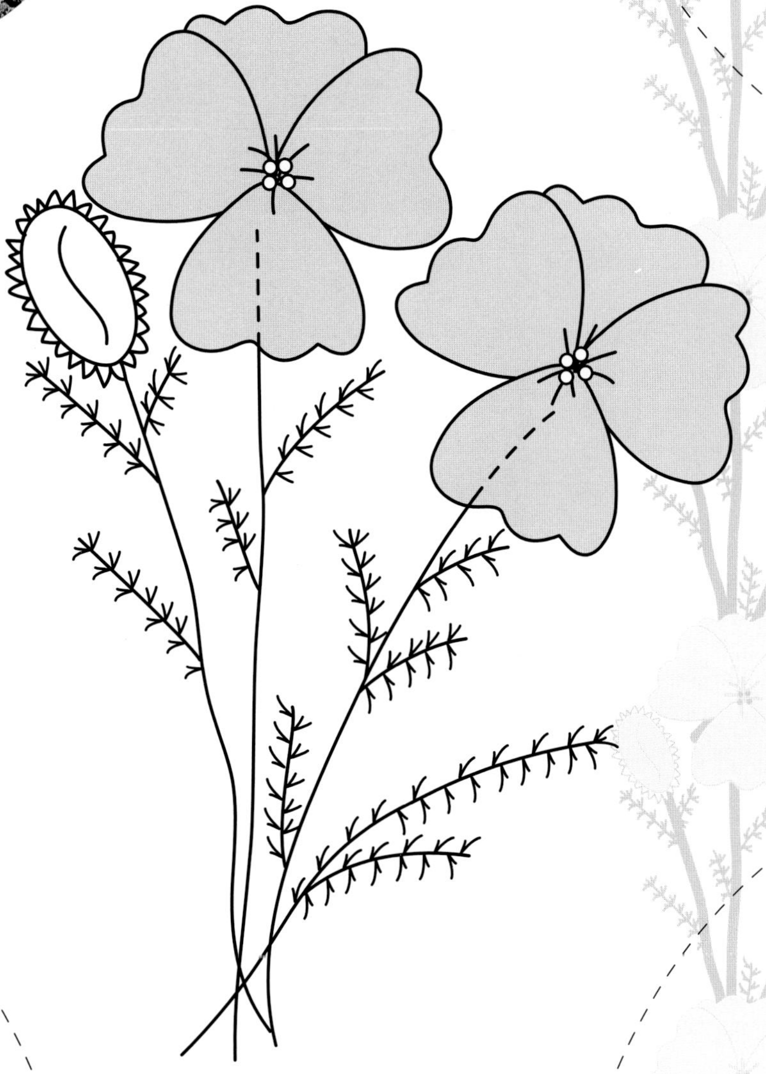

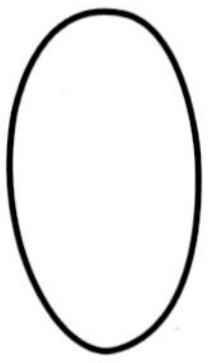

Bud
cut 4
add ³⁄₁₆" turn-under allowance
as you cut

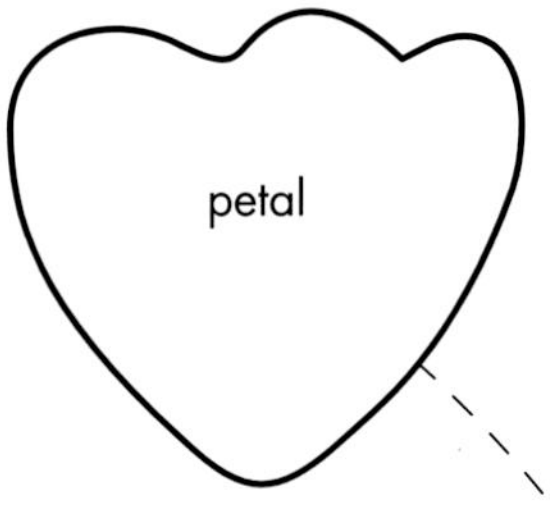

petal

cut 32

Shaded pieces indicate Appli-bond

Forget-me-not &
Queen Anne's Lace
NOSEGAY

Pieced and appliquéd by the author; quilted by Jackie Davis.

Forget-me-not & Queen Anne's Lace

NOSEGAY
traditional block

NOSEGAY

Finished quilt: 58" x 58"
Finished block: 12" x 12"
Number of blocks: 13

You will be sewing two different blocks for this quilt. There are nine traditional Nosegay blocks and four blocks designed to accommodate the Appli-bond flowers.

TEMPLATES
Petal (A)
Cone (B)
Set-in pieces (C & Cr)

FABRIC REQUIREMENTS
The yardage is based on fabric at least 42" wide. You may want to buy a little extra if you like to make sample blocks or if you want a margin for error in rotary cutting.

Fabric	Yards
Petals	scraps
Leaves and inner border	1⅔
Nosegay cone	⅝
Background	2
Outer border and binding	1¾
Backing	3⅝
Batting	62" x 62"

PREPARATION
Cut strips selvage to selvage.

PETALS. Use template A to trace and cut 54 petals from assorted scraps.

LEAVES. First, cut four 1½" inner borders along the fabric length (parallel to selvages). From the remainder, cut two 12⅞" squares. Cut the squares in half diagonally to yield four half-square triangles for the Appli-bond flower background. Trace and cut Template A eight times, also for the Appli-bond background. Then cut 2¼" strips as needed to make 45 – 2¼" squares.

CONE. Cut three 5⅛" strips and layer them, right sides up. Trace and cut 13 pieces from template B (Fig. 2–38).

BACKGROUND. Cut two 2¼" strips, then cut 27 – 2¼" squares from the strips.

Cut three 2¼" strips, then cut strips into 27 – 2¼" x 4" rectangles.

Cut one 3¾" strip into nine 3¾" squares, then cut the squares in half diagonally in both directions to yield 36 quarter-square triangles.

Cut four 3⅛" strips. Use template C to trace and cut 13 pieces (Fig. 2–39). Turn the template over and cut 13 more pieces for Cr.

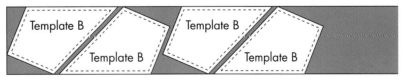

Fig. 2–38.

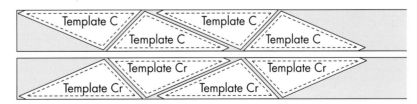

Fig. 2–39.

Fig. 2–40.

Fig. 2–41.

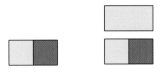

Fig. 2–42.   Fig. 2–43.

Fig. 2–44.

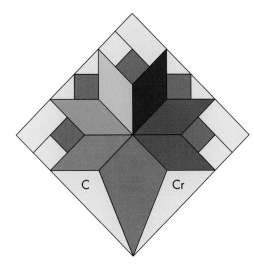

Fig. 2–45.

Cut one 9⅜" strip and cut two 9⅜" squares from the strip. Cut the squares in half diagonally to yield four half-square triangles.

From the remaining 9⅜" strip, cut four 4⅜" squares, then cut them in half diagonally to yield eight half-square triangles for the Appli-bond flower blocks.

Cut two 18¼" squares from one 18¼" strip. Cut the squares on the both diagonals to make eight quarter-square triangles.

OUTER BORDER, BINDING. Cut four 3" border strips the length of the fabric. Cut six 2½" binding strips also lengthwise.

CONSTRUCTION

You will be sewing two different blocks for this quilt. There are nine traditional Nosegay blocks and four Nosegay variations for the Appli-bond flowers.

Traditional Nosegay block:
• Join the scrap petals in pairs (Fig. 2–40).
• For each block, join the pairs and the cone as shown in Fig. 2–41 to complete the nosegay. Make nine nosegays.
• Sew one green 2¼" square to one background 2¼" square (Fig. 2–42).
• Sew a 2¼" x 4" background rectangle to the joined squares (Fig. 2–43) to complete a corner square. Make 27 corner squares for the Nosegay blocks.
• Join one quarter-square background triangle to adjacent sides of a 2¼" green square to make an inset triangle (Fig. 2–44). Make 18 inset triangles, two for each block.
• Sew the three corner squares, two inset triangles, one C, and one Cr to the nosegay to complete the block (Fig. 2–45). Make nine Nosegay blocks.

Nosegay block variation:
• Sew a background quarter-square triangle to a leaf fabric diamond (Fig. 2–46). Make four of these units.
• Reverse the placement of the triangle and the diamond and make four more units (Fig. 2–47).
• Join the triangle-diamond units and the C and Cr background pieces to the nosegay cone (Fig. 2–48). Make four of these Nosegay variations.
• Sew a large leaf fabric half-square triangle to the nosegay unit to complete the block (Fig. 2–49). Make four variation blocks.

Quilt assembly:
• Before joining the blocks to complete the top, appliqué the Forget-me-nots and

Fig. 2–46.

Fig. 2–47.

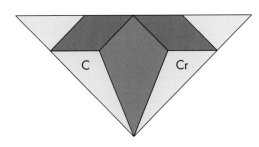

Fig. 2–48.

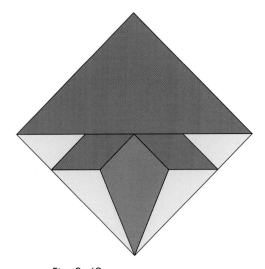

Fig. 2–49.

Queen Anne's lace (page 58) in the center of the Nosegay variation blocks.

• Assemble the quilt blocks in diagonal rows, as shown in the quilt assembly diagram.

• Sew the inner and outer border strips together length-wise before attaching them to the quilt top. Press seam allowances toward the outer border.

• Find the center of each border strip and the center of each quilt edges. Matching centers, pin and sew the border strips in place. Press seam allowances toward the borders. Miter the corners.

• Layer the backing, batting, and quilt top. Baste the layers and quilt them.

• Cut six 2½" strips. Sew them together, end to end with a diagonal seam, to make continuous, double-fold binding. Bind the raw edges to finish the quilt.

At a Glance

Quilt assembly

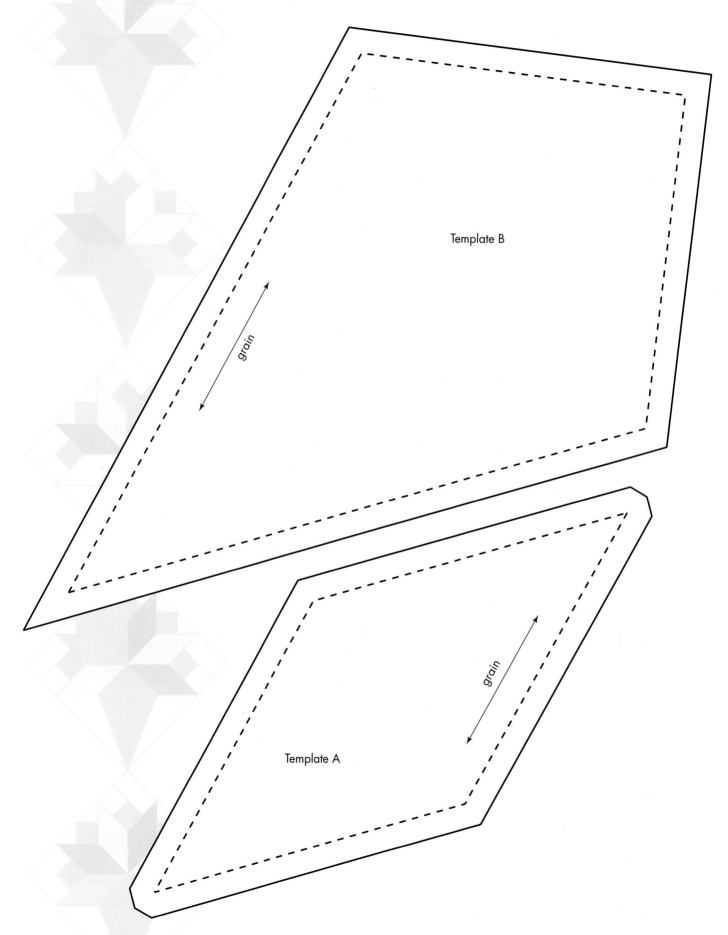

Template B

grain

Template A

grain

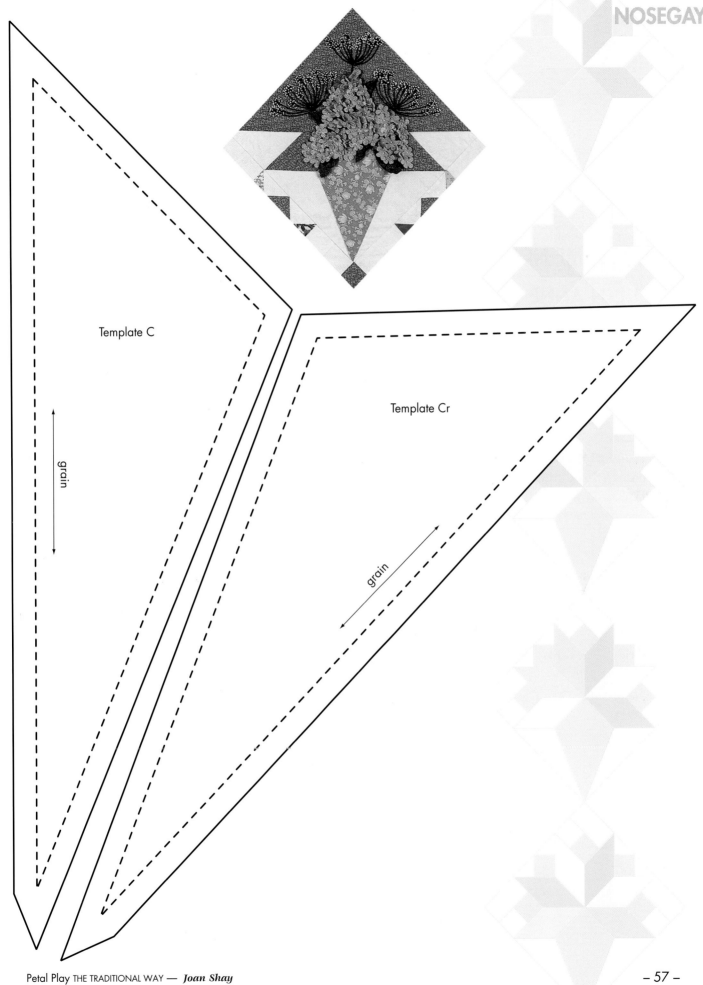

Template C

grain

Template Cr

grain

Forget-me-not & Queen Anne's Lace
NOSEGAY
Appli-bond appliqué

FORGET-ME-NOT and QUEEN ANNE'S LACE

Number of flowers: 4
Flower fits in a 12" x 12" space.

SUPPLIES

HeatnBond UltraHold: 1 yd.
Embroidery floss: green, white, yellow

TEMPLATES

Blossom
Leaf

FABRIC REQUIREMENTS

Blossoms:

Fabric	Yards
Light	½
Dark	½
Leaves	¼

PREPARATION

Appli-bond appliqué:
BLOSSOMS. Cut two light fabric pieces and one bonding piece 12" x 12".

Cut two dark fabric pieces and one bonding pieces 12" x 14".

LEAVES. Cut two fabric pieces and one bonding piece 7" x 12".

Bond the two pairs of blossom fabrics and the two leaf fabrics. Trace the templates on the bonded fabrics and cut 100 light blossoms, 120 dark blossoms, and 20 leaves.

CONSTRUCTION

• Trace the outline of the Forget-me-nots and Queen Anne's Lace on the Nosegay variation blocks. There is no need to trace every blossom. A general outline of the flower head will be sufficient for placing them. Only the stems and branches of the Queen Anne's Lace need to be traced. The French knots are randomly placed.

Queen Anne's Lace:

It is easier to embroider the Queen Anne's Lace before you attach the Forget-me-nots so the embroidery thread won't tangle in the blossoms.

• Embroider the stems and brances with two strands of green embroidery floss and the stem stitch.

• Use two strands of green embroidery floss and the straight stitch to embroider the stamens at the top of each branch (Fig. 2–50)

Fig. 2–50.

• Create the "lace" with French knots made from two strands of white floss. Wrap the needle three times. Randomly place the knots, surrounding the stamens.

Forget-me-nots:

• Thread your Appli-bond needle with two strands of green embroidery floss. Use the stem stitch to attach the bonded leaves to the background by embroidering along the vein lines.

• Attach each blossom to the background with one French knot. (Use two strands of yellow embroidery floss and wrap the Appli-bond needle three times.) Place the blossoms around the outline and gradually fill in the center. Intersperse the light and dark blossoms. You will use about 25 light blossoms and 30 dark blossoms per flower.

• Erase the blue lines with a cotton swab and cold water.

• Heat, curl, and fluff the blossoms.

At a Glance

Templates, p. 10
Appli-bond appliqué, p. 11
Curled petals and leaves, p.12
Embroidery stitches, p. 18

Blossom
cut 100 from light fabric
cut 120 from dark fabric

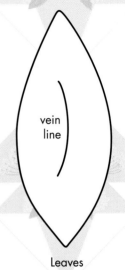

vein line

Leaves
cut 20

General outline for
blossom placement

Shaded pieces indicate Appli-bond

Petal Play THE TRADITIONAL WAY — *Joan Shay*

Shamrock
DOUBLE IRISH CHAIN

Pieced and appliquéd by the author; quilted by Judy Irish.

Shamrock
DOUBLE IRISH CHAIN
traditional block

DOUBLE IRISH CHAIN

Finished quilt: 37½" x 45"
Finished block: 7½" x 7½"
Number of blocks: 30

There are two different blocks that make up this quilt. Strip piecing makes the sewing easy.

FABRIC REQUIREMENTS

The yardage is based on fabric at least 42" wide. You may want to buy a little extra if you like to make sample blocks or if you want a margin for error in rotary cutting.

Fabric	Yards
Background	⅞
Green	½
Purple	⅞
Backing	1½
Binding	½
Batting	41½" x 49"

PREPARATION
Cut strips selvage to selvage.

BACKGROUND. Cut five 2" strips and four 5" strips.
DARK GREEN. Cut nine 2" strips.
PURPLE. Cut sixteen 2" strips.

CONSTRUCTION
Block 1:
Block 1 is made from three strip-pieced units.

UNIT A
• Join five 2" strips in the order shown in Fig. 2–51. Be careful not to stretch the strips as you sew them. Press all seam allowances in the same direction. Make two strip sets.
• Layer the two strip sets right side up and cut them to make 30 – 2" sections.

UNIT B
• Join five 2" strips in the order shown in Fig. 2–52. Make two strip sets.
• Layer the two strip sets right side up and cut them to make 30 – 2" sections.

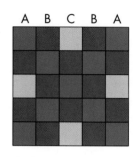

Block 1

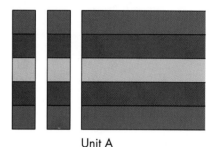

Unit A

Fig. 2–51.

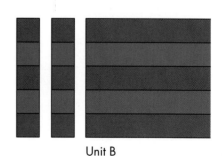

Unit B

Fig. 2–52.

UNIT C

• Join five 2" strips in the order shown in Fig. 2–53. Make one strip set. Cut the strip set into 15 – 2" sections.

• To construct Block 1, sew units A, B, and C as shown in the block diagram. Press seam allowances from the middle outward. Make 15 of these blocks.

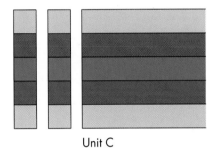

Unit C

Fig. 2–53.

Block 2:

Block 2 is made from two strip-pieced units.

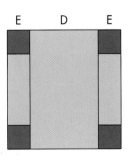

Block 2

UNIT D

• Layer three 5" background strips right side up and cut them into 15 – 8" sections (Fig. 2–54).

UNIT E

• Join 2" and 5" strips as shown in Fig. 2–55. Make two strip sets. Press seam allowances toward the dark fabric.

• Layer the two sets right side up and cut them into 30 2" sections.

• To construct Block 2, sew units D and E as shown in Fig. 2–56. Press seam allowances from the middle outward. Make 15 of these blocks.

• To construct the quilt top, alternate Blocks 1 and 2 as shown in the quilt assembly diagram, page 63.

• Sew the blocks together in rows. Join rows to complete the top.

• Appliqué a Shamrock (page 65) in the center of each Block 2.

• Layer the backing, batting, and quilt top. Baste the layers and quilt them.

• Cut five 2½" strips. Sew them together, end to end with a diagonal seam, to make continuous, double-fold binding. Bind the raw edges to finish the quilt.

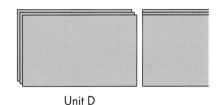

Unit D

Fig. 2–54

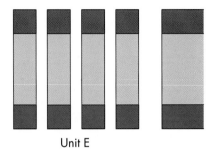

Unit E

Fig. 2–55.

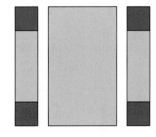

Fig. 2–56.

At a Glance

Quilt assembly

Shamrock
DOUBLE IRISH CHAIN
Appli-bond appliqué

SHAMROCK
(OXALIS)

Number of flowers: 15
Flower fits in a 5" x 9" space.

SUPPLIES
HeatnBond UltraHold: ¾ yd.
Embroidery floss: green
Beads: 45 green, size #6
Nylon bead thread (size D): green

TEMPLATES
Leaf
Blossom

FABRIC REQUIREMENTS

Fabric	Yards
Leaf	½
Blossom	¼
Stems	¼

PREPARATION
Appli-bond appliqué:
BLOSSOMS. Cut two fabric pieces and one bonding piece 8" x 12".

LEAVES. Cut two fabric pieces and one bonding piece 12" x 17".

Bond the two blossom pieces and the two leaf pieces. Trace the blossom and leaf templates on the bonded fabrics and cut 45 blossoms.and 75 leaves.

Traditional appliqué:
STEMS. Cut a 9" strip, then cut ½" bias strips as shown in Fig. 2–57. When ready to appliqué, fold the strips in half lengthwise, wrong sides together. Do not press.

CONSTRUCTION
• Trace the Shamrock in the center of the 15 Block 2s.
• Appliqué the stems to the background.
• Embroider the blossom stems with two strands of green embroidery floss and the stem stitch.
• Attach the bonded leaves to the background by embroidering along the vein lines.

Use your Appli-bond needle, two strands of green embroidery floss, and stem stitch.
• Use your iron to heat each blossom. Cup it in the palm of your hand and shape it over the eraser of a pencil. Hold the shape until it cools.
• Attach the blossoms by sewing a bead in the center then sewing it to the background. Tie the thread securely in the back.
• Curl the leaves by heating them and gently squeezing them between your thumb and index finger.

At a Glance

Cut ½" strips along the length of the fabric.

Fig. 2–57

Blossom
cut 45

Leaf
cut 75

Shaded pieces indicate Appli-bond

Petal Play THE TRADITIONAL WAY — *Joan Shay*

Coneflower
LOG CABIN

Pieced and appliquéd by the author; quilted by Judy Irish.

Coneflower
LOG CABIN
traditional block

LOG CABIN

Finished quilt: 24" x 24"
Finished block: 6" x 6"
Number of blocks: 16

FABRIC REQUIREMENTS

The yardage is based on fabric at least 42" wide. You may want to buy a little extra if you like to make sample blocks or if you want a margin for error in rotary cutting.

Fabric	Yards
Log 1C	⅛
Light log 2L	¼
Remaining light logs	¼ each of 5
Dark logs	¼ each of 6
Backing	⅞
Binding	⅜
Batting	28" x 28"

PREPARATION

Cut strips selvage to selvage.

It is helpful to make a pasted mock-up of the block for fabric placement. Number the logs to save time when constructing the block.

LOG 1C. Cut one 2" strip, then cut that strip into 16 – 2" squares.

REMAINING LOGS. Cut the number of strips indicated, then cut 16 of each log length:

Log	# of strips	Log length
2L	1	1¼" x 2"
3D	2	1¼" x 2¾"
4D	2	1¼" x 2¾"
5L	2	1¼" x 3½"
6L	2	1¼" x 3½"
7D	2	1¼" x 4¼"
8D	2	1¼" x 4¼"
9L	2	1¼" x 5"
10L	2	1¼" x 5"
11D	3	1¼" x 5¾"
12D	3	1¼" x 5¾"
13L	3	1¼" x 6½"

CONSTRUCTION

To sew each block, always lay the pieced unit on top of the log being added, right sides together. Use ¼" seam allowances and press them toward the added log. Square the block after adding each log.

• With right sides together, sew the center square to Log 2L (Fig. 2–58)

• Sew the pieced unit to log 3D (Fig. 2–59). Sew the resulting pieced unit to log 4D (Fig. 2–60). Sew that pieced unit to Log 5L (Fig. 2–61).

• Continue adding logs in this manner until the block is complete (Fig. 2–62). Square the completed block. Make 16 blocks.

• Join four blocks together to make a 12" square with the light logs in the center (Fig. 2–63).

• Add a Coneflower to the center of each 12" square then join the squares to complete the quilt top.

• Layer the backing, batting, and quilt top. Baste the layers and quilt them.

• Cut three 2½" strips. Sew them together, end to end with a diagonal seam, to make continuous, double-fold binding. Bind the raw edges to finish the quilt.

Fig. 2–58.

Fig. 2–59.

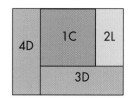

Fig. 2–60.

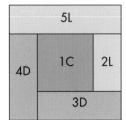

Fig. 2–61.

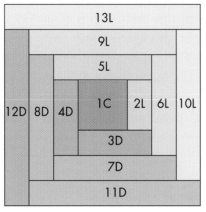

Fig. 2–62.

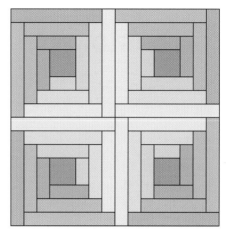

Fig. 2–63.

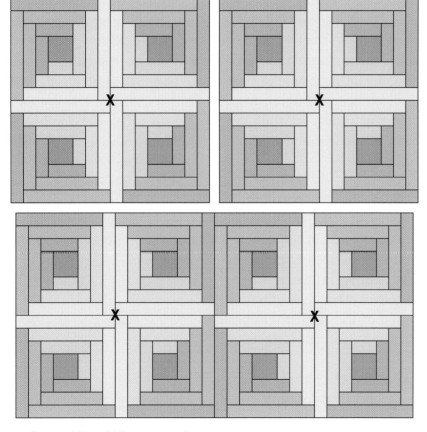

Quilt assembly. Add flower at each X.

KEY

C = center
L = light
D = dark

At a Glance

Machine piecing, p. 15
Backing, p. 20
Layering, p. 21
Quilting ideas, p. 20
Binding, p. 21

Coneflower
LOG CABIN
Appli-bond appliqué

CONEFLOWER

Number of flowers: 4
Flower fits in a 6" x 8" space.

SUPPLIES
HeatnBond UltraHold: ¼ yd.
Embroidery floss: green
Glass beads: #9 (several dozen)
Nylon bead thread: size D

TEMPLATES
Petal
Leaf
Cone

FABRIC REQUIREMENTS

Fabric	Yards
Petals	
(two shades)	⅛ each
Leaves and	
stems	⅛
Cone	⅛

PREPARATION
Appli-bond appliqué:
PETALS. Cut two fabric pieces 4" x 6" for each shade and two 4" x 6" pieces of bonding material.

LEAVES. Cut two fabric pieces and one bonding piece 3" x 5".

Bond the two petal pieces for each shade and the two leaf pieces. Trace the templates on the bonded fabrics and cut 18 petals from each bonded petal fabric and four leaves from the bonded leaf fabric.

Traditional appliqué:
STEMS. Cut four bias strips 1" x 5". Fold strips in half lengthwise, wrong sides together. Do not press.

FLOWER CONE. Trace the template on the right side of the fabric and cut four cones, adding ³⁄₁₆" turn-under allowances by eye as you cut.

CONSTRUCTION
• Use a blue water-soluble pen to trace the outline of the Coneflower in the center of each four-block Log Cabin unit. There is no need to trace every petal. A general outline of the flower will be sufficient for placing the petals.
• Appliqué the stems to the background. Make sure the stems extend under the flow-ers because the petals will lift up.
• Use the stem stitch with two strands of embroidery floss to attach the bonded leaves to the background by embroidering along the vein lines.
• Position the petals on the background with basting glue. Use two stab stitches to attach the petals to the background. The petals will be held more securely once the cone is in place.
• Appliqué the cones. It will be easier to appliqué the bottom portion of the cones if you use an Appli-bond needle because you are sewing through bonded petals.
• Sew beads on the flower cones to achieve a textured appearance.
• Erase the blue lines with a cotton swab and cold water.
• Curl the petals if desired.

= stab stitches

Petal
cut 18
from each bonded fabric

Flower head
cut 4
(add ³⁄₁₆" seam allowance)

Leaves
cut 4
from bonded fabric

Shaded pieces indicate Appli-bond

At a Glance

Morning Glories
FLYING GEESE

Pieced and appliquéd by the author; quilted by Judy Irish.

Morning Glories
FLYING GEESE
traditional block

FLYING GEESE

Finished quilt: 20" x 45"
Finished block: 3" x 6"
Number of blocks: 30

For speedy piecing, the corner-square method is used to make the flying-geese units.

FABRIC REQUIREMENTS

The yardage is based on fabric at least 42" wide. You may want to buy a little extra if you like to make sample blocks or if you want a margin for error in rotary cutting.

Fabric	Yards
Geese	⅔
Background	1⅓
Backing	1½
Binding	⅓
Batting	24" x 49"

PREPARATION

Cut strips selvage to selvage, unless directed otherwise.

BACKGROUND. Cut one center strip 8½" x 45½" the length of the fabric. Cut six 3½" strips across the remaining fabric. From the strips, cut 60 squares 3½".

GEESE. Cut five 3½" strips. Cut 30 rectangles 3½" x 6½" from the strips.

CONSTRUCTION

• Draw a diagonal line on the wrong side of each of the 60 – 3½" background squares (Fig. 2–64).

Fig. 2–64.

• Referring to Fig. 2–65, place a background square, right sides together, on the right end of a rectangle. Make sure the diagonal line runs in the right direction and that the edges of the two pieces are aligned.

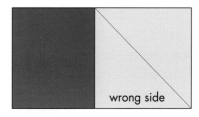

wrong side

Fig. 2–65.

• Sew the square to the rectangle along the drawn line.

• Trim off the corner triangles ¼" from the sewn line (Fig. 2–66). Press the seam allowances toward the triangles. Repeat for all 30 rectangles.

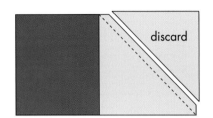

Fig. 2–66.

• In the same manner, use the corner-square method to sew another triangle to the opposite end of each rectangle (Fig. 2–67).

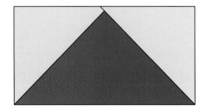

Fig. 2–67.

• Referring to the photo for placement, sew 15 flying geese units together for each side of the quilt. Set aside.

• Appliqué the Morning Glories (page 75) to the center 8½" x 45½" strip.

• Join the two geese strips and the appliquéd strip to complete the quilt top.

• Layer the backing, batting, and quilt top. Baste the layers and quilt them.

• Cut four 2½" strips. Sew them together, end to end with a diagonal seam, to make continuous, double-fold binding. Bind the raw edges to finish the quilt.

At a Glance

Machine piecing, p. 15
Backing, p. 20
Layering, p. 21
Quilting ideas, p. 20
Binding, p. 21

Quilt assembly

Morning Glories
FLYING GEESE
Appli-bond appliqué

MORNING GLORIES

Number of flowers: 4
Flower fits in an 8" x 45"
space.

SUPPLIES
HeatnBond UltraHold: ½ yd.
Embroidery floss: green

TEMPLATES
Blossom
Star shape
Stamen
Small leaf
Large leaf

FABRIC REQUIREMENTS

Fabric	Yards
Three blossom fabrics	⅛ each
White star shape	¼
Green stamen	⅛
Small leaves	¼
Large leaves	¼
Stems	½

PREPARATION
Appli-bond appliqué:
BLOSSOMS. Cut two fabric
pieces from each color and
three bonding pieces, all 9" x
12".

WHITE STAR SHAPE. Cut one
fabric piece and one bonding
piece 9" x 9".

STAMEN. Cut two fabric pieces
and one bonding piece 2" x
4½".

SMALL LEAF. Cut two fabric
pieces and one bonding piece
5" x 9".

LARGE LEAF. Cut two fabric
pieces and one bonding piece
9" x 12".

Bond the fabric pieces for
the blossoms, stamen, and
leaves, but not the star shape.
Trace the templates on the
bonded fabrics and cut four
blossoms of each color, 12
stamens, 12 small leaves, and
16 large leaves.
Bond the wrong side of
the white star-shape fabric.

Do not remove the paper yet.
Trace the star-shaped template on the paper side of the
bonded fabric and cut 12
pieces.
Remove the paper back-
ing and bond a star shape to
each bonded blossom (Fig.
2–68).

Fig. 2–68.

Draw a small circle in the
center of each stamen and
mark as shown in Fig. 2–69.

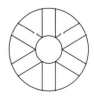

Fig. 2–69.

Cut away the shaded areas
of the bonded stamen as
shown in Fig. 2–70, page 76.

Fig. 2–70.

Fig. 2–71.

Fig. 2–72.

Fig. 2–73.

shown in Fig. 2–70, page 76.

Cut each of the remaining spokes into three thin strips (Fig. 2–71).

Curl each stamen by using an iron to heat each one. Cup the piece in the palm of your hand and shape it over a pencil eraser. Hold the curls until they cool.

Traditional appliqué:

Stems. Cut a 45-degree angle from the ½-yard piece of fabric. Cut two angled strips 1½" by approximately 25" (Fig. 2–72). Join the two pieces to make one long bias strip.

Cut another strip ¾" by approximately 25". When ready to appliqué, fold the strips in half lengthwise, wrong sides together. Do not press.

CONSTRUCTION

• Trace the placement of the vine and blossom stems on the 8½" x 45½" background piece with a blue water-soluble pen. It is not necessary to trace the blossoms and leaves. They can be placed by eye. The vine pattern needs to be traced four times lengthwise to run the length of the quilt top.

• Appliqué the stems (¾" bias strips) to the background.

• Appliqué the vine (1½" bias strip) to the background.

• Use two strands of green floss and the stem stitch to embroider the leaf stems.

• Attach the bonded leaves to the background by embroidering along the vein lines with a stem stitch.

• Heat and curl the small leaves over your index finger. Shape the large leaves by curling them over a pencil (Fig. 2–73).

• To construct the Morning Glories, fold the bonded blossoms (with bonded star shapes) in half, right sides together, and iron a crease. Unfold and fold them in the opposite direction. Press again, being careful not to iron over the previous fold. Reheat one more time and fold the edges of the circle back over your index fingers to shape.

• Layer a prepared stamen in the center of a blossom (glue baste is very helpful) and attach each completed blossom to the background with three French knots in the center of the calyx. Use two strands of green embroidery floss and wrap the Appli-bond needle four times.

• Erase the blue lines with a cotton swab and cold water.

At a Glance

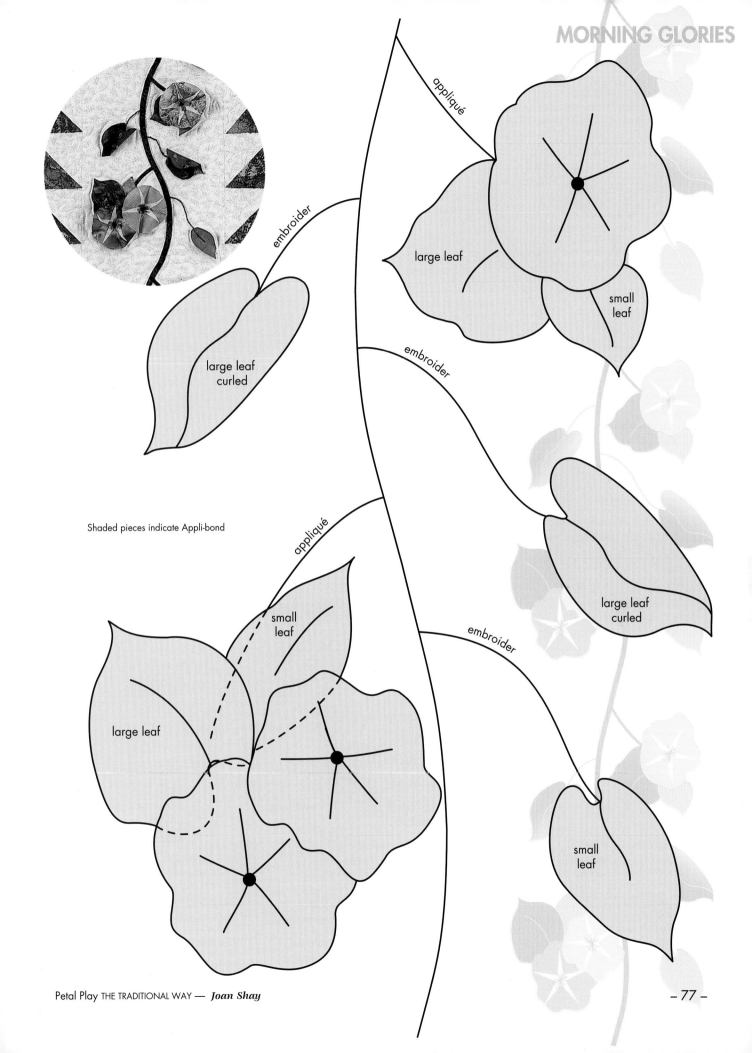

appliqué

embroider

large leaf curled

large leaf

small leaf

embroider

Shaded pieces indicate Appli-bond

large leaf curled

appliqué

small leaf

large leaf

embroider

small leaf

Petal Play THE TRADITIONAL WAY — *Joan Shay*

Star shape
cut 12

Blossom
cut 4 of each color

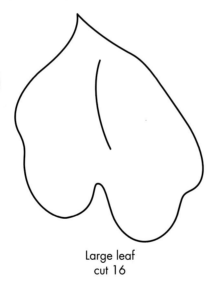

Large leaf
cut 16

Small leaf
cut 12

Stamen
cut 12

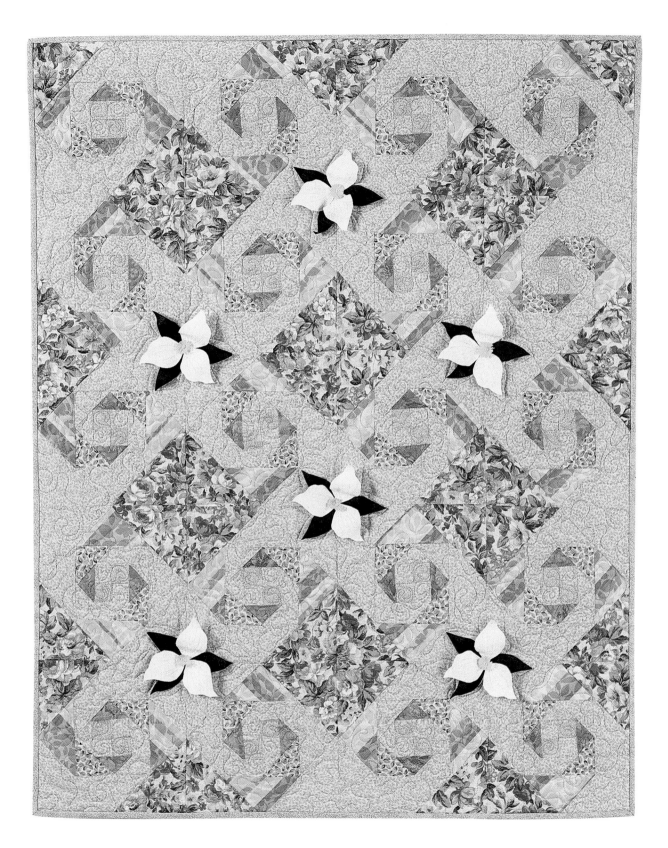

Trillium
SNAIL'S TRAIL

Pieced and appliquéd by the author; quilted by Judy Irish.

Trillium
SNAIL'S TRAIL
traditional block

SNAIL'S TRAIL

Finished quilt: 32" x 40"
Finished block: 8"
Number of blocks: 20

FABRIC REQUIREMENTS

The yardage is based on fabric at least 42" wide. You may want to buy a little extra if you like to make sample blocks or if you want a margin for error in rotary cutting.

Fabric	Yards
Background	1¼
Pink	¼
Green	⅛
Print	¼
Stripe	⅜
Floral	½
Binding	⅜
Backing	1⅜
Batting	36" x 44"

PREPARATION

Cut strips selvage to selvage.

BACKGROUND. Cut two 1½" strips. Cut the strips into 40 – 1½" squares.

Cut two 2¼" strips, then cut 20 – 2¼" squares from the strips. Cut each square in half diagonally to yield 40 half-square triangles.

Cut two 2⅞" strips and cut 20 – 2⅞" squares from the strips. Cut each square in half diagonally to make 40 half-square triangles.

Cut two 3⅝" strips, then cut 20 – 3⅝" squares from the strips. Cut the squares in half diagonally for 40 half-square triangles.

Cut three 4⅞" strips into 20 – 4⅞" squares. Cut each square in half diagonally to make 40 half-square triangles.

PINK. Cut two 1½" strips and cut the strips into 40 – 1½" squares.

GREEN. Cut two 2¼" strips. Cut 20 – 2¼" squares from the strips, then cut each square in half diagonally to make 40 half-square triangles.

PRINT. Cut two 2⅞" strips, then cut the strips to make 20 – 2⅞" squares. Cut each square in half diagonally to make 40 half-square triangles.

STRIPE. Cut two 3⅝" strips and cut 20 – 3⅝" squares from the strips. Cut each square in half diagonally to yield 40 half–square triangles.

FLORAL. Cut three 4⅞" strips into 20 – 4⅞" squares. Cut each square in half diagonally for 40 half-square triangles.

CONSTRUCTION

Press all seam allowances toward the new piece.

• For each block, make a four-patch with two background and two pink 1½" squares (Fig. 2–74).

• Sew two green triangles to opposite sides of the four-patch.

• Sew two of the 2¼" background triangles to the remaining sides of the four patch (Fig. 2–75).

• Following Fig. 2–76, continue to add triangles to opposite sides of the block.

• To join the blocks, it's helpful to arrange the blocks on a flat surface to check for proper rotation and placement.

• Join the blocks in four rows across and five down.

• Appliqué a Trillium (page 82) in the six background areas.

• Layer the backing, batting, and quilt top. Baste the layers and quilt them.

• Cut four 2½" strips. Sew them together, end to end with a diagonal seam, to make continuous, double-fold binding. Bind the raw edges to finish the quilt.

At a Glance

Fig. 2–74.

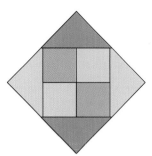

Fig. 2–75.

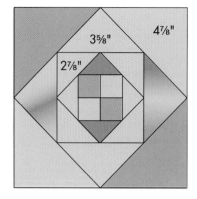

Fig. 2–76.

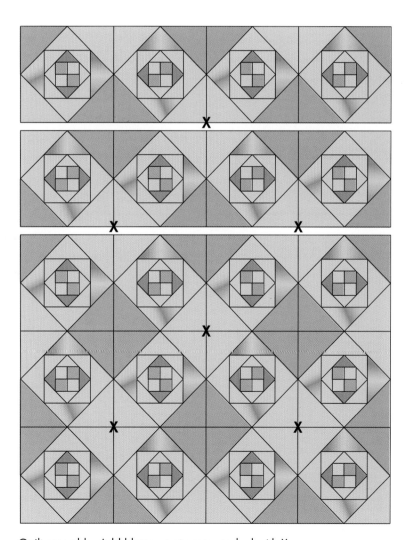

Quilt assembly. Add blossoms at areas marked with X.

Trillium
SNAIL'S TRAIL
Appli-bond appliqué

TRILLIUM

Number of flowers: 6
Flower fits in a 5½" x 5½" space.

SUPPLIES

HeatnBond UltraHold: ½ yd.
Embroidery floss: yellow and green

TEMPLATES

Petal
Flower center
Leaf

FABRIC REQUIREMENTS

Fabric	Yards
Petal	¼
Flower center	scraps
Leaves	¼

PREPARATION

Appli-bond appliqué:
PETALS. Cut two fabric pieces and one bonding piece 9" x 12".

FLOWER CENTERS. Cut two fabric pieces and one bonding piece 2" x 3".

LEAVES. Cut two fabric pieces and one bonding piece 6" x 10".

Bond the fabric pairs for the petals, flower centers, and leaves. Trace the templates on the bonded fabrics and cut 18 petals, six flower centers, and 18 leaves.

On the wrong side of fabric, draw a small circle in the middle of each bonded flower center. Clip the pieces from their outer edges to the drawn circles (Fig. 2–77).

Fig. 2–77.

CONSTRUCTION

• Center the leaves in the six large background areas of the Snail's Trail quilt. Use two strands of green embroidery floss and the stem stitch, sewing a vein in each leaf to attach it to the background.
• Attach the bonded petals to the background with three stab stitches on each. The petals will be held more securely once the flower center is in place.
• Use your iron to heat the bonded flower center and cup it in the palm of your hand. Shape it over the eraser on a pencil.
• Attach the center to the petals with four French knots. Use two strands of yellow embroidery floss and wrap the Appli-bond needle three times.
• Curl the petals by heating them with the iron and gently shaping them over your index finger.

At a Glance

Templates, p. 10
Appli-bond appliqué, p. 11
Curled petals and leaves, p. 12
Embroidery stitches, p. 18

● ● = stab stitches

Petal

Shaded pieces indicate Appli-bond

Flower center

Leaf

Petal Play THE TRADITIONAL WAY — *Joan Shay*

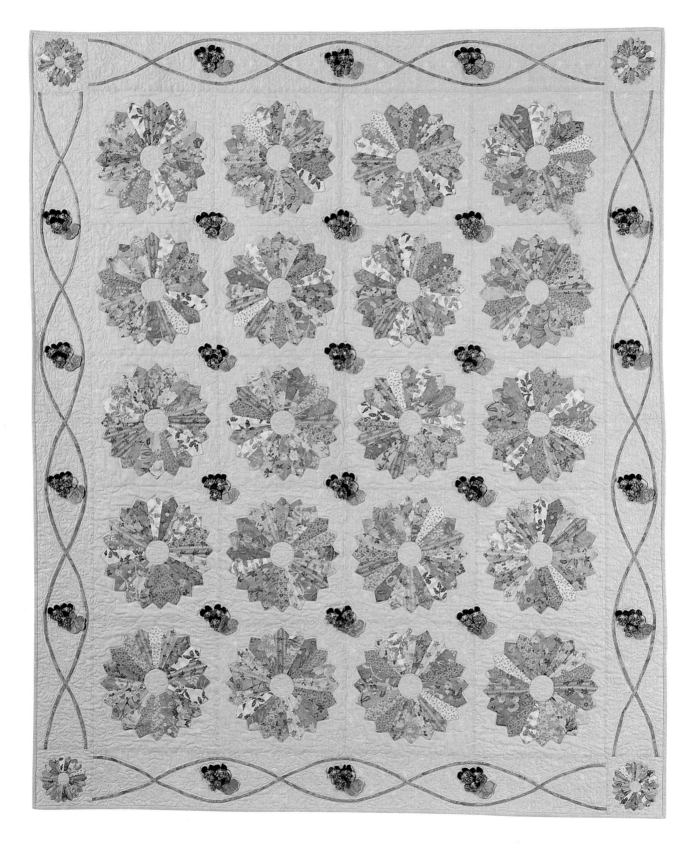

Violets
DRESDEN PLATE

Pieced and appliquéd by the author; quilted by Judy Irish.

Petal Play THE TRADITIONAL WAY — *Joan Shay*

Violets
DRESDEN PLATE
traditional block

DRESDEN PLATE

Finished quilt: 59" x 71"
Finished block: 12" x 12"
Number of blocks: 20

This is a wonderful, easy technique for making Dresden Plates. With little effort, the points are always perfect. I used 20 different fabrics for the wedges and found it more interesting when the colors were placed randomly. I also found that a neutral-colored silk thread was helpful for appliquéing the plates to the background, eliminating the need for frequent thread color changes.

TEMPLATES
Large wedge
Small wedge
Large circle
Small circle
Vine

FABRIC REQUIREMENTS

The yardage is based on fabric at least 42" wide. You may want to buy a little extra if you like to make sample blocks or if you want a margin for error in rotary cutting.

Fabric	Yards
20 plate fabrics	¼ each
Vine	1
Background and binding	4⅝
Backing	3⅝
Batting	40" x 52"

PREPARATION

Cut strips selvage to selvage, unless directed otherwise.

BACKGROUND. First, cut a 62" length from the yardage. From this piece, cut four 6" wide border strips lengthwise (parallel to the selvages). Cut four 12½" blocks from the remainder of this piece.

Cut six 12½" strips across the remaining yardage (selvage to selvage). Cut 16 more 12½" squares and four 6" corner squares from the strips.

PLATES. Layer five plate fabrics at a time, all right sides up, and cut a 4½" strip across the width of the fabrics.

Trace the large wedge, alternating its position as shown in Fig. 2–78, and cut 20 wedges through all layers. Trace the small wedge four times, and cut the pieces through the five layered fabrics.

Repeat the cutting instructions three more times to make 400 large wedge pieces and 80 small ones.

VINE. Cut enough 1" bias strips to equal 14 yards in length.

BACKING. Piece the backing horizontally (Fig. 2–79).

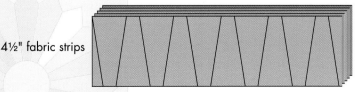
4½" fabric strips

Fig. 2–78.

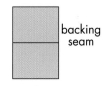
backing seam

Fig. 2–79.

trim to ⅛" →

fold

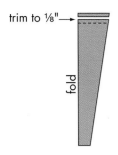

Fig. 2–80.

Fig. 2–81.

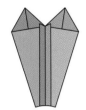

Fig. 2–82.

Fig. 2–83.

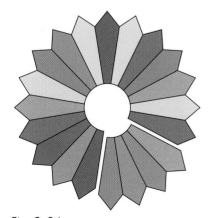

Fig. 2–84.

CONSTRUCTION

Each plate contains 20 wedges. Accurate ¼" seam allowances are important for the success of the block.

• Fold a wedge in half lengthwise, right sides together. Starting at the fold, sew a ¼" seam across the wide end. Trim that allowance to ⅛" (Fig. 2–80). Repeat to prepare 20 wedges for each plate.

• Open the wedge, forming a sharp point and press the point and folded edges carefully (Fig. 2–81).

• Sewing from the wide end to the narrow end, right sides together, join wedges in pairs (Fig. 2–82). Press allowances open to reduce bulk.

• Join pairs into units of four wedges (Fig. 2–83). Each plate consists of five units of four wedges.

• Join the units to form a circle (Fig. 2–84). Make 20 large and four small plates (6" block).

• Center each plate on a background square. Baste it in place and appliqué around the outside edge.

• Center the large circle template on each appliquéd plate and trace with a blue water-soluble pen.

• Turn the inside raw edges under, to the blue line, and appliqué in place. You may need to open some of the seams to the line to form a smooth, flat circle.

• Erase the blue lines with a cotton swab and cold water.

• Join the completed 20 large blocks, four across and five down.

• Appliqué 12 bouquets of violets (page 90) at the intersections of the blocks.

• For each border strip, mark a ¼" seam line at both ends.

• Align the vine template center line with the seam lines of each border and trace the template with a blue water-soluble pen (Fig. 2–85).

• Continue tracing the vine the length of the border, placing the template point to point (Fig. 86). The short borders will have three whole and two half vine motifs. The longer borders will have four whole and two half vines. Appliqué the vines to the border strips.

• Erase any blue lines with a cotton swab and cold water.

• Appliqué a violet bouquet in the center of each vine.

• Sew the longer border strips to the sides of the quilt.

• Sew a completed small Dresden Plate block to each end of the remaining border strips. Attach the borders to the quilt top and bottom.

• Layer the backing, batting, and quilt top. Baste and quilt.

• Cut seven 2½" strips. Sew them together, end to end with a diagonal seam, to make continuous, double-fold binding. Bind the raw edges to finish the quilt.

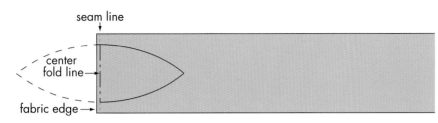

seam line

center
fold line →

fabric edge →

Fig. 2–85.

At a Glance

Machine piecing, p. 15
Backing, p. 20
Layering, p. 21
Quilting ideas, p. 20
Binding, p. 21

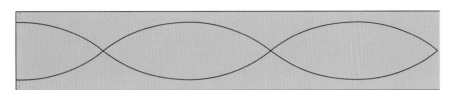

Fig. 2–86.

Quilt assembly

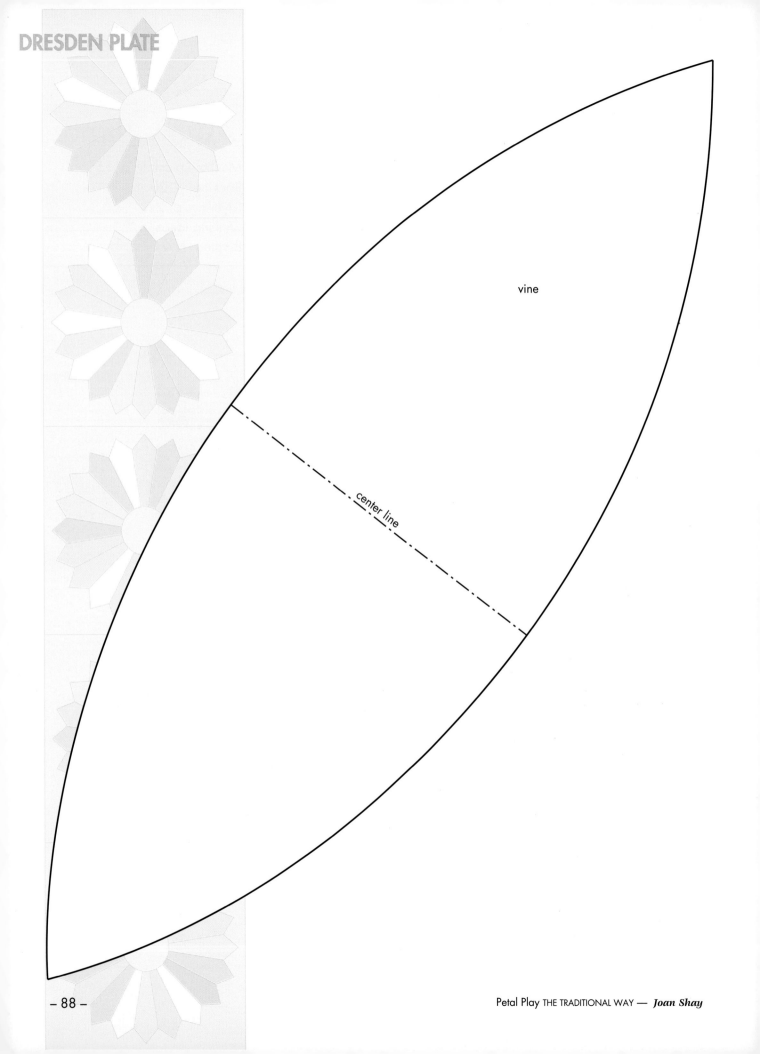

vine

center line

Petal Play THE TRADITIONAL WAY — *Joan Shay*

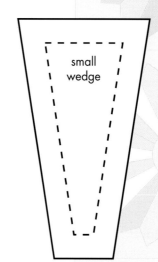

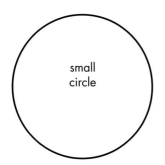

small
circle

small
wedge

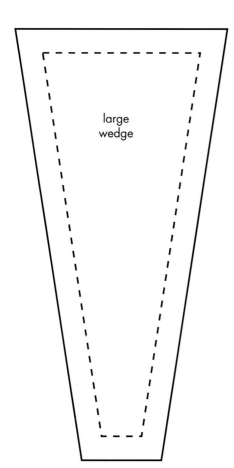

large
wedge

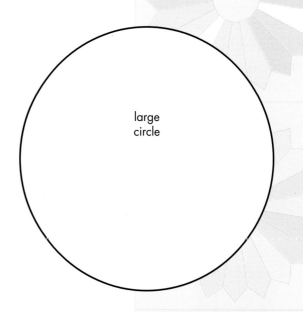

large
circle

Violets
DRESDEN PLATE
Appli-bond appliqué

VIOLETS

Number of flowers: 26
Flower fits in a 5" x 5" space.

SUPPLIES
HeatnBond UltraHold: ¾ yd.
Embroidery floss: yellow and green

TEMPLATES
Upper petal
Lower petal
Leaf

FABRIC REQUIREMENTS

Fabric	Yards
Dark violet	¼
Medium violet	¼
Leaves	¼

PREPARATION
Appli-bond appliqué:
PETALS. Cut two dark upper petal pieces and one bonding piece 9" x 17".

Cut two medium lower petal pieces and one bonding piece 9" x 17".

LEAVES. Cut two fabric pieces and one bonding piece 9" x 17".

Bond the fabric pairs for the petals and leaves. Trace the templates on the bonded fabrics and cut 78 dark violet petals, 78 medium violet petals, and 26 leaves.

Curl the petals by heating them with an iron and shaping them over your index finger.

Use a stab stitch or glue basting to attach two petal pieces together as shown in Fig. 2–87.

Embroider the center of each blossom before attaching it to the background. Use two strands of yellow floss and the straight stitch.

Fig. 2–87.

CONSTRUCTION
• Use a blue water-soluble pen to trace the outline of the violet pattern on the Dresden Plate quilt top. The violets in the borders are centered in the vines.
• To attach the bonded leaves to the background, use two strands of green floss and the stem stitch to embroider along the vein lines (Fig. 2–88).
• Embroider the stems with two strands of embroidery floss and the chain stitch.
• Attach the violet blossoms to the background with three yellow French knots. (Use two strands of floss and wrap the Appli-bond needle three times.)
• Erase the blue lines with a cotton swab and cold water.

Fig. 2–88.

Petal Play THE TRADITIONAL WAY — *Joan Shay*

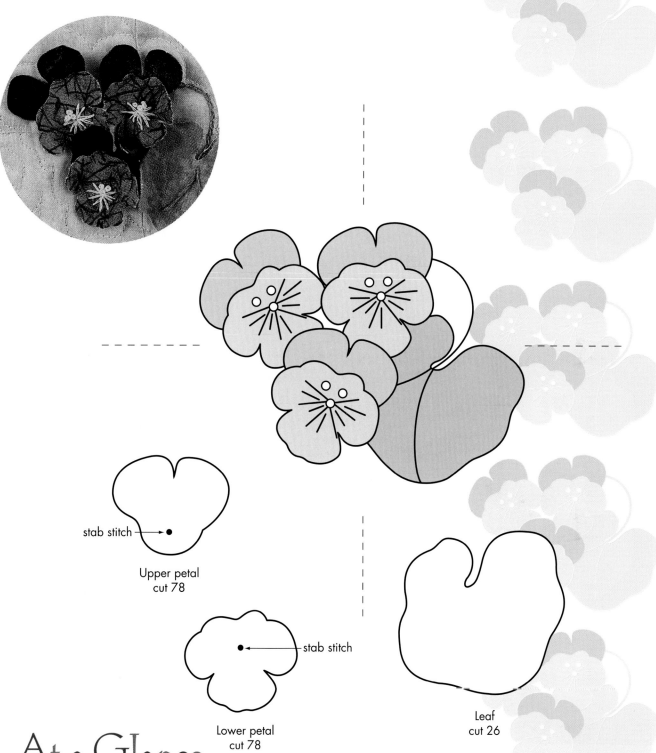

stab stitch →●

Upper petal
cut 78

●→ stab stitch

Lower petal
cut 78

Leaf
cut 26

At a Glance

Templates, p. 10
Appli-bond appliqué, p. 11
Curled petals and leaves, p. 12
Embroidery stitches, p. 18

Shaded pieces indicate Appli-bond

Christmas Cactus
SNOWBALL

Pieced and appliquéd by the author; quilted by Judy Allen.

Christmas Cactus
SNOWBALL
traditional block

SNOWBALL

Finished quilt: 36" x 36"
Finished block: 6"
Number of blocks: 25

Instructions are given for the corner-square technique, a fast, accurate way of adding half-square triangles to the Snowball block. This technique is also used in the Flying Geese Quilt.

FABRIC REQUIREMENTS

The yardage is based on fabric at least 42" wide. You may want to buy a little extra if you like to make sample blocks or if you want a margin for error in rotary cutting.

Fabric	Yards
White	⅞
Red	1½
Backing	1¼
Batting	40" x 40"

PREPARATION

Cut strips selvage to selvage.

WHITE. Cut four strips 6½". Layer the strips right side up and cut 25 – 6½" squares from the strips.

RED. For the corner triangles, cut seven 2½" strips. Layer the strips right side up and cut to make 100 – 2½" squares. Do not cut the squares in half.

For the vertical sashing, cut four 1½" strips.

Cut six 1½"-wide horizontal sashing strips and trim them to 34½".

For the side sashing, cut two strips 1½" x 36½".

CONSTRUCTION

• For the corner triangles, draw a diagonal line on the wrong side of each of the 100 2½" squares (Fig. 2–89).

Fig. 2–89.

• Place a 2½" square on one corner of a white 6½" square, right sides together (Fig. 2–90). Make sure the diagonal line is angled in the right direction and that the edges of the two pieces are aligned.

Fig. 2–90.

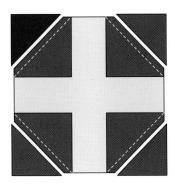

Fig. 2-91.

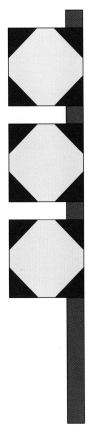

Fig. 2-92.

• Sew the corner square to the snowball (6½")square along the drawn line. Repeat for all four corners on all 25 – 6½" squares.

• Trim the extra triangles from the corner squares, leaving a ¼" seam allowance from the sewn line (Fig. 2-91). Press seam allowances toward the darker corner triangles.

• Chain sew 20 Snowball blocks to the sashing strips (Fig. 2-92). Sew with the sashing strip underneath. (Note that five Snowball blocks will not be sashed). Press seam allowances toward the sashing. Trim and square up the blocks, as shown in Fig. 2-93.

• Join one unsashed block and four sashed blocks to complete a row (Fig. 2-94). Make five rows.

• Join the rows with the horizontal sashing strips and press. Add the side sashes to complete the quilt top (see quilt assembly diagram).

• Appliqué the Christmas Cactus (page 96) to the completed snowball top.

• Layer the backing, batting, and quilt top. Baste the layers and quilt them.

• Cut four 2½" strips. Sew them together, end to end with a diagonal seam, to make continuous, double-fold binding. Bind the raw edges to finish the quilt.

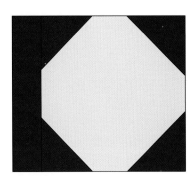

Fig. 2-93.

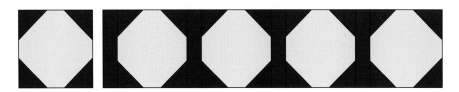

Fig. 2-94.

Quilt assembly

Petal Play THE TRADITIONAL WAY — *Joan Shay*

Christmas Cactus
SNOWBALL
Appli-bond appliqué

CHRISTMAS CACTUS

Cactus fits in an 18" x 18" space.

SUPPLIES

HeatnBond UltraHold: 1 yd.
Wax paper

TEMPLATES

Cactus
Flower
Folded bud
Flowerpot

FABRIC REQUIREMENTS

Fabric	Yards
Cactus	¾
Flowers and buds	¾
Flowerpot	¼

PREPARATION
Appli-bond appliqué:

CACTUS PIECES. Cut two fabric pieces and one bonding piece 17" x 22".

Cut one piece for the patches shown in Fig. 2–96 and one bonding piece 6" x 17".

FLOWERS. Cut two flower pieces and one bonding piece 12" x 12".

Bond the fabrics for the cactus pieces and the flowers. Trace the templates on the bonded fabrics and cut 18 cactus pieces and 10 flowers.

Bond the patch fabric by applying the bonding material to only one side of the fabric.

Cut the bonded patch fabric into two 1½" x 17" strips. Cut the strips into 17 – 1½" squares.

When cool, remove the paper backing.

ROLLED BUDS. From the flower fabric, cut two ½" strips the width of the fabric.

Layer the strips and cut eight ½" x 6" rectangles.

Construct eight rolled bud, following the instructions on page 17. Notice that these rolled buds are fairly long, so you may need to tack some of the folds with invisible thread or basting glue. Five of these buds will be used for constructing the flowers.

FOLDED BUDS. Trace the folded bud template on the flower fabric and cut nine pieces on the line. No seam allowance is necessary. Construct nine folded buds, following instructions on page 18.

FLOWERPOT. Trace the template on the flowerpot fabric and cut one piece, adding a ³⁄₁₆" turn-under allowance by eye as you cut.

CONSTRUCTION

• Cut a small "x" in the center of each flower (Fig. 2–95).

Fig. 2–95.

• Use your iron to heat each flower. Shape one petal at a time to form a cup.

• Push a rolled bud halfway through the "x" cut in one flower. Push the bud through a second flower, about a quarter of the way this time. The cup of the flower should point away from the tip of the rolled bud. Make five compound flowers.

• Place a bud on the end of one cactus piece with the end of the bud overlapping the cactus by ½". Place a piece of wax paper on your ironing surface to protect it, then bond a 1½" patch square over the end of the cactus and the bud (Fig. 2–96).

• When the patch is cool, trim the patch to match the shape of the cactus piece (Fig. 2–97). Repeat the instructions to attach the remaining flowers and buds to the cactus ends.

• Some of the cactus pieces are branches of others and extend from under them. Use two strands of embroidery floss, the Appli-bond needle, and the stem stitch to join the pieces, as shown in Fig. 2–98. Cactus pieces 14–18 will be attached only part way to allow them to fall forward.

• Following the placement diagram for the Christmas cactus, attach the cactus pieces to the Snowball top in numerical order (Fig. 2–99, page 98).

• Appliqué the flowerpot to the background. It will be necessary to stab stitch the top of the pot because it is too difficult to appliqué through the bonded material.

Fig. 2–96.

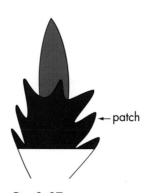

Fig. 2–97.

Fig. 2–98.

At a Glance

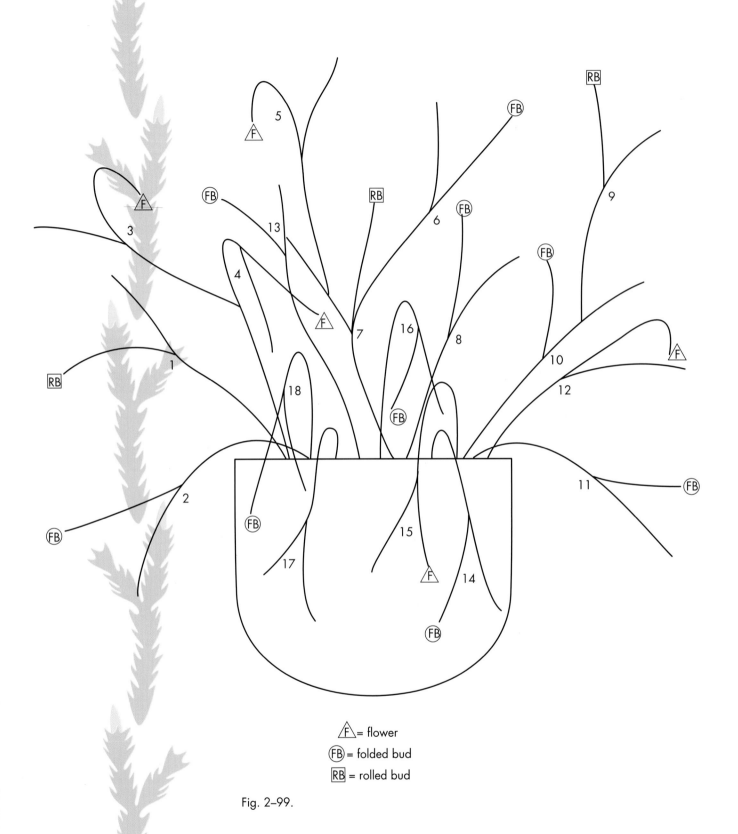

F = flower

FB = folded bud

RB = rolled bud

Fig. 2–99.

Flower
cut 10

Cactus
cut 18

CHRISTMAS CACTUS

flowerpot
cut 1
add ³⁄₁₆" turn-under allowance

folded bud
cut 9
(no seam allowance)

Petal Play THE TRADITIONAL WAY — *Joan Shay*

Chapter 3
CHALLENGE GALLERY

SUNFLOWER MYSTERY, made by Marie Pedlow, Somers, New York. Marie used the Wheel of Mystery block with the Appli-bond Sunflower.

Challenges are a big part of many quilt guild programs. Each challenge has different guidelines and rules, and the results are always surprising.

When planning this book, I decided to issue a challenge to many of my friends and former students. I asked them to make quilts by combining traditional blocks with my Appli-bond flowers.

Petal Play THE TRADITIONAL WAY — *Joan Shay*

(FACING PAGE). A PLACE FOR ELEANOR, made by Mary Beth Larsen, Geneva, New York. Mary Beth used the Pinwheel block with the Appli-bond Magnolia.

(TOP, LEFT). The Cathedral Window blocks and Appli-bond Calla Lilies were used in this quilt made by Wendy F. Strumwasser, Plainview, New York, and the author.

(TOP, RIGHT). BOUNTIFUL GRAPES, made by Mary Hayes, Auburn, New York. Mary used the Grape Basket block with Appli-bond Grapes.

(BOTTOM). GRAPES OF WRATH, made by Meg Mooar, Stanford, Connecticut. Meg used the Drunkard's Path block with Appli-bond Grapes.

Petal Play THE TRADITIONAL WAY — *Joan Shay*

(FACING PAGE). LILACS IN THE WIN-
DOW, made by Wendy F.
Strumwasser, Plainview, New York.
Wendy used the Cathedral Window
block with the Appli-bond Lilac.

(ABOVE). PRIMROSE PATH, made by
Glenda LePage, Lakeside, Connecticut. Glenda used the Drunkard's Path
block with the Appli-bond Primrose
and Jack-in-the-Pulpit.

(RIGHT). WEDDING RING PANSIES,
made by Dorothy Scalice, New Mil-
ford, Connecticut, and quilted by Judy
Irish. Dorothy used the Wedding Ring
block with the Appli-bond Pansy.

(TOP, LEFT). GRANDMERE'S MEMORIES, made by Debbianne Prussman, Dennisport, Massachusetts. Debbianne used the Crazy Quilt block with the Appli-bond Holly Wreath, Poinsettia, Amaryllis, and Mistletoe.

(TOP, RIGHT). REDWORK DAISIES, made by Adelaide Chandler, Skaneateles, New York. Adelaide used Redwork on the Appli-bond Daisy pattern.

(LEFT). CABIN PRIMROSE, made by Adelaide Chandler, Skaneateles, New York. Adelaide used the Log Cabin block with the Appli-bond Primrose.

(FACING PAGE). PRIMROSE TRAIL, made by Jo Coon, Cicero, New York. Jo used the Snail's Trail block with the Appli-bond Primrose.

Petal Play THE TRADITIONAL WAY — *Joan Shay*

Petal Play THE TRADITIONAL WAY — *Joan Shay*

FOUR SEASONS Wallhanging, made by Emily Farrell Koon, Marcellus, New York. Emily use the Basket block and the Appli-bond Magnolia, Tulip, Poinsettia, and Grapes.

Home Shopping

Special contacts and products are listed below. Check your local quilt shop for product availability before contacting companies directly.

Company	Products and services

PETAL PLAY
Joan Shay
102 Courtney Rd.
   Harwich, MA 02645
508-430-0347
www.petalplay.com
	Workshops, lectures,
	Appli-bond needles, straw needles,
	   pattcrns, books, templates, HeatnBond

HANCOCK FABRICS 381 Hinkleville Rd. Paducah, KY 42001 www.Hancocks-Paducah.com	Fabrics, notions
HEARTBEAT QUILTS Helen Weinman 765 Main St. Hyannis, MA 02601 800-393-8050 www.heartbeatquilts.com	Fabric, kits and quilting supplies
BETTY KISER 4531 Bibb Dr. Millbrook, AL 36054 www.getcreativeshow.com/path_less_traveled.htm	Drunkard's Path books, curved templates
QUILTING FROM THE HEARTLAND Sharlene Jorgenson PO Box 610 Starbuck, MN 56381 www.qheartland.com	Double Wedding Ring books, acrylic templates
ROXANNE INTERNATIONAL 85 Tuscany Way Daneville, CA 94506 www.thatperfectstitch.com	Glue-Baste-It

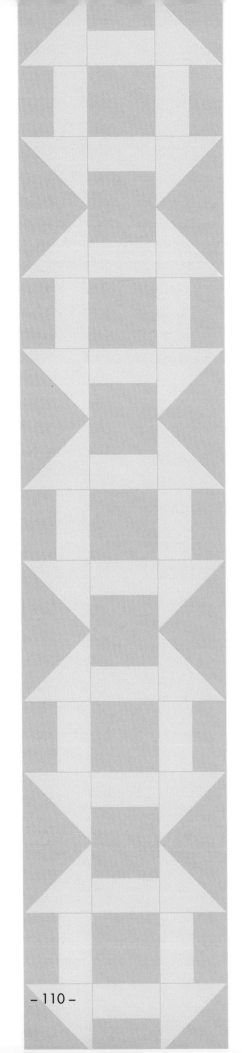

Suggested Books

Burns, Eleanor. *Irish Chain in a Day*. San Marcos, CA: Eleanor Burns, 1986.

Hanson, Joan. *Sensational Settings*. Bothell, WA: That Patchwork Place, Inc., 1993

Hargrave, Harriet. *Heirloom Machine Quilting*. Martinez, CA: C&T Publishing, 1990.

Johnson-Sebro, Nancy. *Rotary Magic*. Emmaus, PA: Rodale Press, Inc., 1998.

Jorgenson, Sharlene. *Double Wedding Ring*. Starbuck, MN: Sharlene Jorgenson, 1997.

Kiser, Betty. *The Path Beyond*. Carlisle, PA: Betty Kiser, 1994.

Leman, Bonnie and Judy Martin. *Taking the Math Out of Making Patchwork Quilts*. Wheatridge, CO: Moon Over the Mountain, 1981.

Martin, Judy. *Scrap Quilts*. Wheatridge, CO: Moon Over the Mountain, 1985.

McClun, Diana and Laura Nownes. *Quilts! Quilts!! Quilts!!!* Lincolnwoods, IL: Quilt Digest Press, 1988.

Miller, Phyllis. *Sets & Sashings for Quilts*. Paducah, KY: American Quilter's Society, 2000.

Montano, Judith. *Elegant Stitches*. Lafayette, CA: C&T Publishing, 1995.

Wolfrom, Joan. *Make Any Block Any Size*. Lafayette, CA: C&T Publishing, 1999.

About the Author

Although Joan doesn't love gardening, she does love flowers. It was through her love of flowers and a desire to make them as realistic as possible out of fabric that her Appli-bond technique was conceived. It's difficult to believe that she comes to quilting having no artistic training because her Petal Play designs are so life-like.

Joan, who was taught to sew on a Singer treadle machine by her grandmother, has been a quilter for many years. She has her own pattern company, Petal Play, which she operates from her home in Massachusetts. In addition, she has taught and lectured extensively throughout the country. She has appeared on television on the PBS show "Quilting from the Heartland" with Sharlene Jorgenson, and on the HGTV program "Simply Quilts" with Alex Anderson.

A registered nurse, Joan and her husband, Tony, live on Cape Cod. They have two children, Matthew and Kristin and a grandaughter, Shay Elizabeth.

Other AQS Books

This is only a small selection of the books available from the American Quilter's Society. AQS books are known worldwide for timely topics, clear writing, beautiful color photos, and accurate illustrations and patterns. The following books are available from your local bookseller, quilt shop, or public library.

#5848   US$19.95

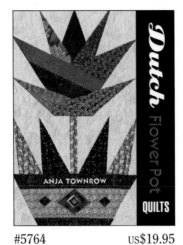

#5764   US$19.95

#5844   US$21.95

#5705   US$22.95

#5013   US$14.95

#5709   US$22.95

#5760   US$18.95

#5851   US$18.95

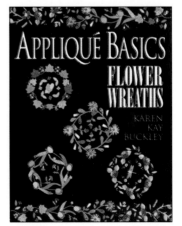

#5335   US$21.95

Look for these books nationally or call **1-800-626-5420**